DONNA WALKER TILESTON

What Every Teacher Should Know About
SPECIAL LEARNERS

W0008376

CORWIN PRESS
A Sage Publications Company
Thousand Oaks, California

Copyright © 2004 by Corwin Press

For information:

Corwin Press
A Sage Publications Company
2455 Teller Road
Thousand Oaks, California 91320
www.corwinpress.com

Sage Publications Ltd.
6 Bonhill Street
London EC2A 4PU
United Kingdom

Sage Publications India Pvt. Ltd.
B-42, Panchsheel Enclave
Post Box 4109
New Delhi 110 017 India

Printed in the United States of America

Library of Congress Cataloging-in-Publication Data

Tileston, Donna Walker.
What every teacher should know about special learners /
Donna Walker Tileston.
    p. cm. — (What every teacher should know about—; 8)
Includes bibliographical references and index.
ISBN 0-7619-3124-4 (Paper)
    1. Special education—United States—Handbooks, manuals, etc.
2. Children with disabilities—Education—United States—Handbooks,
manuals, etc. I. Title. II. Series.
LC3981.T53 2004
371.9′043—dc21   2003012384

This book is printed on acid-free paper.

        04   05   06   07   10   9   8   7   6   5   4   3

Acquisitions Editor:	Faye Zucker
Editorial Assistant:	Stacy Wagner
Production Editor:	Diane S. Foster
Copy Editor:	Stacey Shimizu
Typesetter:	C&M Digitals (P) Ltd.
Proofreader:	Mary Meagher
Indexer:	Molly Hall
Cover Designer:	Tracy E. Miller
Production Artist:	Lisa Miller

Contents

About the Author

Donna Walker Tileston, Ed.D., is a veteran teacher of 27 years and the president of Strategic Teaching and Learning, a consulting firm that provides services to schools throughout the United States and Canada. Also an author, Donna's publications include *Strategies for Teaching Differently: On the Block or Not* (Corwin, 1998), *Innovative Strategies of the Block Schedule* (Bureau of Education and Research [BER], 1999), and *Ten Best Teaching Practices: How Brain Research, Learning Styles, and Standards Define Teaching Competencies* (Corwin, 2000), which has been on Corwin's best-seller list since its first year in print.

Donna received her B.A. from the University of North Texas, her M.A. from East Texas State University, and her Ed.D. from Texas A & M University-Commerce. She may be reached at www.strategicteachinglearning.com or by e-mail at dwtileston@yahoo.com.

Acknowledgments

My sincere thanks go to my Acquisitions Editor, Faye Zucker, for her faith in education and what this information can do to help all children be successful. Without Faye, these books would not have been possible.

I had the best team of editors around: Diane Foster, Stacy Wagner, and Stacey Shimizu. You took my words and you gave them power. Thank you.

Thanks to my wonderful Board Chairman at Strategic Teaching and Learning, Dulany Howland: Thank you for sticking with me in the good times and the tough spots. Your expertise and friendship have been invaluable.

To my sister, Sandra Kay Barnhart, who has dedicated much of her adult life to the field of nursing.

**CORWIN
PRESS**

The Corwin Press logo—a raven striding across an open book—represents the happy union of courage and learning. We are a professional-level publisher of books and journals for K-12 educators, and we are committed to creating and providing resources that embody these qualities. Corwin's motto is "Success for All Learners."

Introduction

Goals of Schoolwide Education Reform

- *Challenging standards for all students*
- *Resources targeted to students with the greatest academic needs, in amounts sufficient to make a difference*
- *A focus on teaching and learning, with components aligned and working together to help every student meet the standards*
- *Partnerships among families, communities, and schools to support student attainment of high standards*
- *Administrative flexibility to stimulate school-based initiatives, coupled with accountability for student performance*

—U.S. Department of
Education, September 1997

These reforms express my deep belief in our public schools and their mission to build the mind and character of every child, from every background, in every part of America.

—President George W. Bush on
the No Child Left Behind Legislation

Anyone who studies the history of education knows that, where there are education issues, reform cannot be far behind. As educators, we are constantly seeking ways to improve upon our methodology and on the final product—our students. We will not be content until every child is successful.

I have never been an administrator in a school that had less than 100% mastery as its goal. The problem with setting a goal that is anything less than 100% is that it assumes there will be failures. Even a mastery level of 85% assumes that 15% of the students will not be successful. The question becomes, "Who are the students in the 15%—is it my child? Is it yours?" As a former administrator once told me, "Casualties are light unless you are one of them."

Throughout this book, you will find ideas for making students more successful in the classroom. All of the teaching and learning practices offered have a strong research base and have the power to make a difference in children's lives.

One of the most important things that we can do to prepare students for success on tests is to teach the vocabulary of the test. Form 0.1, below, provides the vocabulary that will be examined throughout this book. Look at the words to see which ones are familiar and which are not. Write your own definitions in the middle column, and adjust your thinking as your read through this book.

I have also provided a pre-test on the vocabulary that will be used throughout this book. The Vocabulary Summary at the end of the book contains the terms and their definitions. Once you have finished the book, you will be given a second chance to show what you know on a vocabulary test.

Form 0.1   Vocabulary List for Special Learners

Vocabulary Word	Your Definition	Your Revised Definition
Achievement test		
Assessment		
At-risk		
Auditory impairment		
Autism		
Battery of tests		
Bloom's taxonomy		
Consent		
Content		
Creative and productive thinking		
Criteria		
Cumulative record		
Curriculum compacting		
Deaf/blind		
Differentiation		
Due process		
Early childhood		
Emotional disturbance (ED)		
Gifted education		
Guardian		
Homebound program		
Inclusion		
Individual Education Plan (IEP)		
Individual Education Plan (IEP) Committee		

(Continued)

Form 0.1 Continued

Intelligence quotient (IQ)		
Learning disability (LD)		
Least restrictive environment (LRE)		
Mainstream		
Mental age		
Mental retardation (MR)		
Modality		
Multiple disability		
Occupational therapy (OT)		
Orthopedic impairment		
Physical therapy (PT)		
Process		
Product		
Public Law 94-142		
Reinforcement		
Related service		
Self-contained classroom		
Special education		
Speech and language therapy		
Speech impairment		
Surrogate parent		
Traumatic brain injury		
Visual impairment		

Vocabulary
Pre-Test

Instructions: For each question given, choose the best answer or answers. More than one answer may be correct.

1. Martin Phillips is a new teacher at the ABC Middle School. Recently, while in the teachers' lounge, he heard a teacher say that she was attending an IEP meeting for a student who was LD. He quickly excused himself and went to his book on special populations so that he could look up the terms. Which of the following would he likely find?
   A. An IEP meeting is a meeting to determine the socioeconomic status of the student.
   B. An IEP meeting is a meeting to determine the best way to serve a special education student.
   C. An IEP meeting usually results in an IEP.
   D. Only special education staff attends an IEP meeting.

2. As Martin Phillips read, he found the following information to be correct:
   A. LD students are no different from students served under Title I.
   B. LD students are protected under PL 94-142.
   C. LD students need diagnostic and prescriptive feedback.
   D. LD students are usually ADD as well.

3. Students who have been identified as gifted . . .
   A. Usually do well without intervention
   B. Can be served through curriculum compacting
   C. Can be served by giving them additional work
   D. Need opportunities to work together

4. Students who are identified as LD . . .
   A. Have an IQ and an achievement level at about the same range
   B. Have an average or above-average IQ
   C. Have problems with basic skills
   D. Have low IQ scores

5. Public Law 94-142 . . .
   A. Was written to provide services to gifted children
   B. Was written for disabled children
   C. Ensures free services for special populations
   D. Ensures pull-out programs for gifted children

6. For purposes of special education placement, a child who has no parents will be assigned a . . .
   A. Guardian
   B. Special education person to represent them
   C. Surrogate parent
   D. Principal or teacher to represent them

7. Felipe is a middle school student who receives special education services. An IEP for Felipe has been given to his classroom teachers. At a minimum, Felipe can expect what?
   A. His parents signed the IEP before it was presented to the teachers.
   B. His teachers were involved in the IEP.
   C. His teachers will follow the guidelines to the letter.
   D. His goals will be reviewed every three years.

8. Martina speaks little English and is being served by a program to help her to be successful in school. What are some things that we can count on that are being done for Martina?

A. She is served by an LPAC.

B. She is served by an LEP program.

C. She is served by special education.

D. Everyone in her school has been trained to work with students like Martina.

9. Blindness is identified at . . .

A. 20/60, with correction

B. 20/80, with correction

C. 20/100, with correction

D. 20/200, with correction

10. Differentiation in the classroom is accomplished through . . .

A. Content

B. Process

C. Compacting

D. Products

11. Which of the following criteria are used in identifying students as at risk?

A. They are English language learners.

B. They have low socioeconomic status.

C. They have experienced previous failure in basic skills.

D. Ethnicity.

12. An ADD student typically has which of the following characteristics?

A. Shows off

B. Is withdrawn

C. Is bossy

D. Is inattentive

13. An ADHD student typically has which of the following characteristics?

A. Is bossy

B. Shows off

C. Does not bond with friends

D. Is withdrawn

14. The modality most often found in school is . . .
    A. Multimodal
    B. Auditory
    C. Visual
    D. Kinesthetic

15. Second language acquisition intervention includes . . .
    A. ELL students
    B. ESL students
    C. LEP students
    D. Students who use casual register

16. IDEA . . .
    A. Is a program for gifted students
    B. Is a program for after-school services
    C. Is a federal legislation
    D. Is a program for LEP students

17. An IEP is. . .
    A. A program for after-school services
    B. A program for differentiating instruction
    C. A program for gifted students
    D. A program for Section 504 students

18. Section 504 . . .
    A. Provides services for special education students
    B. Provides services for gifted education
    C. Provides services for students outside the special education perimeters
    D. Provides services for all students

19. The definition of such disorders as ADHD comes from . . .
    A. Title I
    B. APE
    C. DSM-IV
    D. FERPA

20. The No Child Left Behind Act differs from previous
    legislation in that it calls for . . .
    A. Greater flexibility in the use of funds
    B. Strong research background in teaching techniques
    C. More accountability
    D. More choices for parents

1

Differentiation and the Brain

Differentiation is the use of time, planning, and instructional practices to meet the different needs of diverse learners. Tomlinson (1999) says, "In differentiated classrooms, teachers begin where students are, not the front of a curriculum guide." The classroom teacher has the task of differentiating curriculum every day in order to meet the needs of all of the learners. Special populations, which include at-risk students, special education students, and gifted students, all need that differentiation if they are to be successful.

Some of the special populations that we will discuss in this chapter and the chapters to follow include those students—

1. Identified as needing the services of a program for academically gifted

2. Identified as having Attention Deficiency Disorder (ADD) or Attention Deficiency Hyperactive Disorder (ADHD)

3. Identified for services under the guidelines of special education

4. Identified for services under at-risk guidelines including guidelines for English language and second language learners, compensatory education, Section 504, and Title I

5. Identified for services under emotional and behavioral services

THE BRAIN IN ACTION

In order to understand the needs of these students and how the classroom teacher can modify and differentiate for those differences, it is necessary to look at how the brain learns, processes, and retrieves information under most circumstances. According to Sprenger (2002), we identify as "smart" those students who can take in information efficiently and quickly, process it, and then retrieve it quickly when it is needed. Gifted students tend to process more efficiently and quickly, and thus they need modifications so that they are challenged sufficiently and can reach their potential. Students with learning or behavioral problems may not be able to carry out one or more of these functions (taking in information, processing it, and retrieving it) without difficulty.

Incoming Information

It has been said that smart people are those who can quickly store and retrieve information. Underachievers are those who process information quickly but retrieve it from storage slowly; overachievers are those who process information slowly but retrieve it from storage quickly. How, then, can we help students process information in a faster and more efficient way so that when they need to use the information they can retrieve it quickly?

Our rate of learning is the amount of time it takes to acquire information. Using the graphic in Figure 1.1, let's look at how the brain takes in information, how it decides what to keep and what to discard, and how it retrieves information from long-term memory.

Figure 1.1   A Summary View of the Learning Process, From the Senses to Retrieval

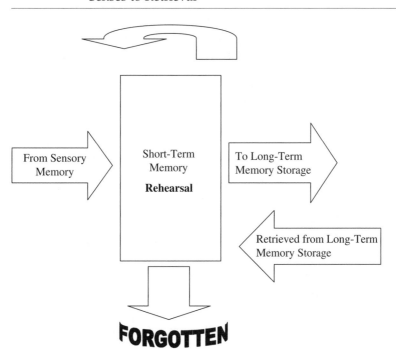

Most brain researchers say that 99% of what we learn comes to us through our senses—vision, hearing, smelling, tasting, and feeling. That means that the classroom environment is important and that the way teachers teach students is important in getting information processing in the brain. For students experiencing difficulty with the learning, the classroom environment is a critical part of the learning process for them. How can we help these students to use their senses to take in information at a more efficient rate and to move the information to the processing center of the brain?

Using a Variety of Learning Modalities

Researchers have identified three learning modalities most often used by students to taking in information. Most of us prefer one of these modalities to the others and are able to take in information faster and more efficiently if taught in our preferred modality. As a matter of fact, it is believed that students who have difficulty with the learning will not be successful unless they are re-taught in the modality in which they learn best. Following is a discussion of the three modalities and their characteristics (from Tileston, 2000).

Visual Learners. Visual learners make up the largest group in the classroom; perhaps as many as 87% of the students in any given classroom are visual learners. These students need to "see" the learning: Memorizing formulas in math is not enough for them. They need to know how the math works and they need to see it visually. Many of our at-risk students can be moved to higher levels of understanding simply by adding visual tools to the learning. Both linguistic and nonlinguistic tools are the keys to working with these learners.

Visual learners are those students who:

- Have difficulty remembering names but may remember details about a person
- Learn best when there are visual tools to help explain the learning
- Would rather read a story than have someone tell it to them
- Organize thoughts by writing them down
- Have difficulty remembering directions that are told to them
- Facial expressions often give away their emotions
- Like puzzles

As teachers, we can help these students to be more successful by using visual models. Visual models are usually either linguistic (i.e., use words to communicate the information) or nonlinguistic (i.e., use structure, symbols and fewer words to communicate the information). Form 1.1 is an example of a nonlinguistic organizer that helps students to organize the information in their notebooks.

Form 1.1   Linguistic Organizer

Mathematical Principle	Example	Notes to Help Me Remember

Students with learning problems are usually not very well organized, yet they need the structure to help them learn. For these students, it is essential that the classroom teacher set up structures to help these students organize their work. The structure in Form 1.1 is set up for a math notebook so that students can keep up with the different math concepts and formulas and how they are used. For language arts, a similar chart might be included for vocabulary words or parts of speech. For science, how to read the periodic table might be put into a graphic format.

An example of a nonlinguistic organizer is provided in Figure 1.2. A nonlinguistic organizer relies on structure and few words to help students learn.

The brain likes structure. As a matter of fact, the brain builds new learning by attaching it to old learning or experiences. When we can put information into a structure, we help all learners, but especially at-risk learners, to understand the information. In studies conducted by Mid-continent Regional Educational Laboratory and written by Marzano (1998), the effect size of using graphic models to help learners was significant. This means that students working at the 50th percentile range who receive instruction that includes visual

Figure 1.2   Nonlinguistic Organizer

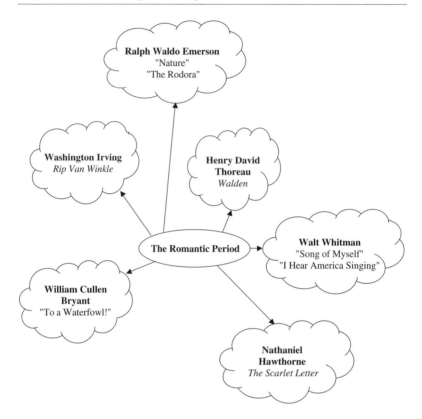

graphic models can make as much as 39 percentile points progress when the instructional strategy is used properly. In other words, a student at the 50th percentile range can be moved to the 89th percentile range through the appropriate use of visual models. While this information comes from studies with regular education students, the studies conducted under the auspices of the U.S. Department of Education (2002) conclude that practices that make a significant difference in the learning of regular education students will probably make a significant difference for all students.

For students with visual perception problems or poor experiences with the learning, visuals will only be helpful if they are discussed in detail by the teacher or by others. Guenther (1998) says that what we see is really not a direct representation of reality but one based on inferences within our brains based on past experience and perceptions. Given (2002) provides the following example:

> Two students may react quite differently to a poster showing various brain lobes and an announcement that the next thematic science unit will focus on the nervous system. A student with low reading skills and limited success in science may perceive only portions of the poster that accentuate his weaknesses. He immediately believes that his skills are inadequate to the task, fails to see any positive aspects of the project, and responds with worry. By contrast, another student, whose background is richly endowed, may perceive abundant detail and look forward to the experience as an exciting new learning opportunity.

Auditory Learners. Auditory learners make up the smallest number of the learners in the classroom. Many veteran teachers are auditory learners and were taught in classrooms that relied on lecture and discussion for learning. Few of today's students learn that way, which explains why many students struggle in a classroom based solely on lecture for disseminating information. It is not unusual to find in these classrooms that only a small percentage of the students are successful—usually those students who are auditory and those students that are good at adapting to the mode of teaching being used at any time. Most at-risk students are not good at adapting to the teaching style of the classroom.

Students who are auditory learners:

- Remember names better than faces
- Forget what is read unless it is discussed
- Would rather be in a group discussion about a topic than to read about it
- Are easily distracted by sounds
- Are good storytellers

For these students it is important that they hear the learning. Information does not have meaning to them until they hear the words and repeat them. Peer tutoring, discussions, and oral lessons are good tools for these students.

According to Given (2002), "Children with auditory processing deficit may have adequate hearing but have a great difficulty distinguishing the differences between sounds such as /b/,/d/,/g/,/p/,/t/, or /v/ and /f/." This may be the result of frequent ear infections from birth to three years of age. Given says that these children need intervention as soon as possible in phonemic awareness, "before a single collective neural net becomes firmly entrenched and similar sounds are perceived as one. The child must be aware that fine discriminations are necessary to grasp the appropriate meaning of language heard." She suggests using preschool alphabet books and playing "I see something you don't see and it begins with a B" as ideas for helping these students make the discriminations in sounds.

Kinesthetic Learners. Kinesthetic learners are those students who need movement and tactile approaches to the learning. They learn best when they can touch the information. Models and manipulatives are good tools for these learners. Many ADD and ADHD students come under this classification. By providing opportunities for these students to move and to experience the learning, the classroom teacher will assist these learners to understand the learning.

Some characteristics of kinesthetic learners include the following:

- They remember best what was done, rather than what is seen or talked about.
- When faced with a problem, they will often choose the solution that involves the greatest activity.
- They would rather participate in an event than to watch it.
- Their body language is a good indicator of their emotions.

- They like to build models.
- They like simulations, drama, and outdoor activities.
- They need movement or they may become a discipline problem.

Once information enters the brain through the senses, about 98% is discarded by the brain as not relevant. There are, however, some things that we can do as teachers to assist the brain to make good choices.

Processing Information

On test day students will often come into the classroom and say, "Hurry, hurry and give me the test before I forget the information." Those students do not know the material; they are merely saying it over and over (about every 15 seconds) so that they can hold it in working memory long enough to write it on the test. Ask them the same question next week and they will not remember the information. Once information enters the working memory (sometimes called *short-term memory*), we have about 15 seconds while the brain decides to process the information or to discard it: About 98% is discarded.

How, then, do we ever move information into long-term memory? The key to getting information into long-term memory is rehearsal (see Figure 1.3).

Rehearsal refers to what we do with the information once it has been introduced into working memory through the senses. Rehearsal performs two functions: it maintains information in short-term memory and it is the mechanism by which we transfer information to long-term memory. Both the amount of time devoted to the rehearsal and the type of rehearsal are important. Rehearsal may be rote or elaborate.

Rote rehearsal is deliberate, continuous repetition of material in the same form in which it entered short-term memory. Rote rehearsal is used when the learner needs to remember

Figure 1.3   The Road From Input to Discard

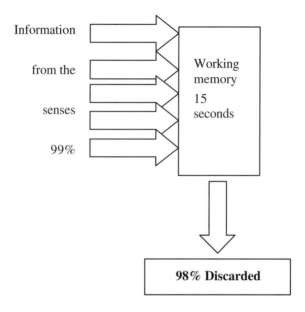

and store information exactly as it is entered into working memory. Examples of material learned by rote include math facts, spelling, and state capitals.

Elaborative rehearsal involves elaborating on or integrating information, giving it some kind of sense or meaning. In elaborative rehearsal, the learner does something with the information. Elaborative rehearsal is used when it is not necessary to store information exactly as learned, but when it is more important to associate the new learnings with prior learnings to detect relationships. Examples of material learned by elaborative rehearsal include problem solving, vocabulary in context, and reading comprehension.

Think about your classroom: What do you have students *do* with new information? We cannot create meaning for our students, but we can facilitate the process through good instructional practices. Most researchers agree that there are three basic ways that we make meaning:

- *Through relevance*—Jensen (1997) says, "In order for learning to be considered relevant, it must relate to something the learner already knows. It must activate a learner's existing neural networks. The more relevance, the greater the meaning."
- *Through emotion*—Emotion is the strongest force for embedding information into long-term memory; it has the power to shut down our thinking or to strengthen an experience so that we remember it for life. We add emotion to the learning through music (try adding sounds of the times to lessons), celebrations of the learning, adding visuals and simulations, and real-world applications.
- *Through patterns or connections*—The brain is a seeker of connections; it is constantly asking, "What do I already know about this subject that can be connected?"

STORING AND RETRIEVING INFORMATION

Although there is controversy over the number of memory pathways that we have, most researchers agree that there are three primary memory pathways. Let's review them in terms of how to help students to use them more effectively.

Semantic Memory

The semantic memory (also known as *taxon, declarative, categorical,* or *linguistic memory*) is the system most often used in education. It is the area that stores words and facts—and it is the least brain-compatible of the three memory systems. That is one of the reasons our students cannot remember the learning. Sprenger (1999) says,

New information enters the brain through the brain stem, goes to the thalamus, and is then sent to the hippocampus, which is the file cabinet for factual memories. If incoming sensory information is factual, it will use the hippocampus to search its files for matching information. The brain will look for prior learning or experiences with which to connect the new learning. It may take several tries for the brain to do this. Anything that we can do as teachers to facilitate this process will help our students to make sense of the information.

We can lead our students to the connections or, if there is not prior learning, provide a connector for our students. For example, for a lesson on the Romantic period, I may have students who are not familiar with the works of Emerson, Irving, Thoreau, and Whitman, but they are probably familiar with the idea of romance. I might start the unit by asking my students to list for me the characteristics of romance. From that list, I might lead my students to the understanding that in romance, we tend to have a preference for emotion over reason or logic. That, of course, is one of the characteristics of the literature of the Romantic Period.

When facts and words are taught in isolation without any context or connection, they are lost unless rehearsed, reviewed, or relearned. Teaching English language learners using the semantic memory system is unproductive, because these students lack the language to be able to make meaning of the learning. The same is true of students from poverty, since most of their learning outside of school and prior to entering school has been contextual and has involved the semantic memory system in only a very limited way.

Jensen (1998) says,

> The exact location of the semantic memory function has not been pinpointed, though we know it operates out of the cerebral cortex. The brain is poorly designed for remembering print and text copy. Information embedded in content is usually learned, or attempted to be learned, through rote tactics and by following list-like formats. Semantic memory is the type of list-oriented, sometimes rote, memory which requires rehearsal; it is resistant to

change, is isolated from context, has strict limits, lacks meaning and is linked to extrinsic motivation.

In other words, if students are to learn facts and words, they must have something with which to connect that information, otherwise it is useless to the brain and discarded. Some ideas that help students to remember facts or words include mnemonics (e.g., Please Excuse My Dear Aunt Sally for mathematical operations), rhymes (e.g., the alphabet with a song), peg words, or with similar content (e.g., "Last week we learned X. This week we will add to that by learning . . ."). As Jensen (1997) says, "This type of learning is typified by seated classroom work and homework, e.g., 'Study for Friday's test by reading Chapter Six.'"

Semantic memory is related to chunks of information. We can only handle a few chunks at one time. The number of chunks of information that we can process at one time is age dependent and fixed (i.e., we cannot change the number of chunks, although we can change how much we put into a chunk). LeDoux (1996) says that adults—those with a mental age of 15 and up—can hold up to seven items in short term memory at one time. Sprenger (1999) says, "Beginning at age three a child has one memory space. Every other year this increases by one space until the capacity of seven is reached. Then two spaces can be either added or subtracted, depending on interest level and prior knowledge." Form 1.2 shows the chunks by age.

The more that we can put information into manageable chunks or categories for our students, the more information they can deal with at one time. I can teach 20 items to my students at one time if I can find a way to put that information into chunks. For example, instead of having students memorize a list of reasons for World War II, a teacher is more likely to help students remember if the reasons are put into categories, such as economic reasons, legal reasons, and social reasons. Random lists of vocabulary are easier to learn if the information is put into categories. Prior to a lesson, provide a

Form 1.2   Chunking

Memory Space (+/– 2)

Age	Number of Chunks
15–adult	7
13	6
11	5
9	4
7	3
5	2
3	1

list of vocabulary and possible categories for students to determine the categories based on what they already know about the vocabulary (see Form 1.3). Provide opportunities throughout the learning for students to revise their list.

Episodic Memory

The episodic memory system (also known as *contextual, loci,* or *spatial memory*) is based on context and location (i.e., where you were when you learned the material or in what context you learned the information). While this memory system is used in the early elementary years, its use diminishes each year as the student moves through the education system, until it is rarely used in secondary school except in the arts or vocational classes.

This memory system, located in the hippocampus, is highly brain-compatible and can be remembered for years (although details may become distorted unless they are reviewed from time to time). Sprenger (1999) says, "The

Form 1.3   Teaching Students to Develop Categories (i.e., "Chunks")

Directions: Cut out the list of words below and decide which are categories. Place the vocabulary words under the appropriate categories. You may make your own categories as well.

Adrenaline	Automatic memory	Frontal lobe
Midbrain	Neocortex	Peptide
Structure of the brain	Memory pathways	Stress chemicals
Types of memory	Semantic	Cell membrane
Procedural	Contextual	Amygdala

---

important link for this memory lane is that you are always somewhere when you learn something so you can easily associate the learning with the location."

This is the memory pathway that stores information taught from the bulletin board, the chalkboard, or a color-coded sheet of paper—anything that gives the information context. During a test, you may see students look at the covered-up bulletin board in an attempt to recall the information that was there. If you ask a student a question for which they do not know the answer, sometimes just saying, "Remember, it was on the blue vocabulary sheet" can help trigger this memory lane. We tend to do better on tests when we take the test in the same room that we learned the information. Think about how we often conduct national or state tests by taking students to the lunchroom or some other general place. Try putting the students back into the classrooms for standardized tests. If your students are typical of those in studies conducted by Jensen (1998), your students will do better on the test. Using visuals can help students to use this memory system more effectively. Remember that at least 87% of learners need visuals.

It is this memory system that allows us to remember where we were when significant events in history took place, such as the death of Dr. Martin Luther King or President Kennedy, or the explosion of the space shuttle. The episodic memory is also why this generation will remember 50 years from now where they were on September 11, 2001. Contextual learning is essential as we work with students from poverty. These students often lack the vocabulary skills to learn in the semantic system but have experience in learning through story telling, which is a part of the episodic memory system.

Teachers who work with students from poverty will do well to explore this memory system and how to incorporate it into the classroom. Since students today are often not motivated intrinsically, this is a good memory system, because it requires little intrinsic motivation to be activated. By combining this memory system with the words and facts needed in the semantic memory system, teachers can help students not only to review information but also to remember it.

Finally, the episodic memory system has unlimited storage capacity. Where the semantic memory system is limited by chunks (7–10 for an adult), the episodic memory system requires little intrinsic motivation to remember and can remember large amounts of information for years—forever, if the information is rehearsed periodically.

Some examples of ways to use the episodic memory system include the following:

- Post information so that it is visually accessible to the learners who need visuals to learn. For English language learners, visuals are critical to their learning because they have limited semantic acquisition strategies.
- Color-code units, especially if there is a great deal of vocabulary involved.

- Use graphic (i.e., nonlinguistic) organizers to help students "see" the learning and teach students to develop graphic organizers of their own for learning.
- Change the room arrangement prior to a new unit. Doing so affects context ("Remember, we talked about that information when you were all seated facing the windows").
- Use symbols and/or costumes to help students separate the learning. I use picture frames (what I call "frames of reference") when studying the Romantic Period in literature. One group of students has a frame that says *Emerson*, another a frame that says *Hawthorne*, another one that says *Whitman*, and so forth. Each group must talk about their author in terms of how he or she used the characteristics of the Romantic Period in his or her writing. The frame serves as a context for the learning.

Procedural Memory

The procedural memory (also called *body, motor,* or *kinesthetic memory*) is powerful memory system stored in the cerebellum. It seems to have unlimited capacity (as opposed to the semantic memory, which is limited by chunks), and we tend to remember the information stored there for years. Jensen (1997) says, "Procedural memory, also known as motor memory, includes that which happens when one, for example, learns to ride a bicycle, remembers the melody of a favorite song (musical memory) and recalls the fragrance of a flower (sensory memory)."

Sprenger (1999) calls it muscle memory, because it has to do with what the body does and remembers. It is strongly brain-compatible. Material learned this way is highly likely to be recalled; in fact, this method is the most commonly used for early childhood learning. A child's life is full of actions, which require him or her to stand, ride, sit, try out, eat, move, play, build, and run. The learning is then embedded in the body, and therefore remembered.

Students from poverty have had many experiences learning this way. If they want to know something, they generally learn by doing it. Adding movement to the learning is a great way to reach these students, as well as ADD and ADHD students. As a matter of fact, teachers trying to work with students from poverty or students with ADD or ADHD by teaching through lecture (i.e., by accessing the semantic memory system) are setting themselves and the students up for failure.

You can add movement to the lessons through the following:

1. Role-playing

2. Drama

3. Choral reading

4. Projects

5. Hands-on activities

6. Manipulatives

7. Debates

8. Group activities

Other Memory Systems

Tileston (2000) and Sprenger (2002) say you will find two other memory systems listed. Some researchers, such as Jensen (1998), say that although we first thought there were five memory systems, two of those systems are probably part of the original three. The two memory systems sometimes mentioned are the automatic and emotional memory systems.

Automatic memory. Automatic memory is also found in the cerebellum and is sometimes called *conditioned–response memory* because the automaticity is a result of conditioning. Some examples of where this system is used include multiplication tables, the alphabet, and decoding skills. The use of flashcards or songs in order to learn facts are ways of putting information into the automatic system. Researchers, such as Jensen (1998), say that the automatic memory is really a part of the procedural memory system.

Emotional Memory. Sprenger (2002) says,

> This memory lane begins with the amygdala, the limbic structure that sifts through all incoming information for emotional content. The amygdala is very powerful and can take control of the brain. For this reason, attaching emotional memories to learning can make a tremendous difference in how material is remembered. The primary emotions are joy, fear, surprise, sadness, disgust, acceptance, anticipation, and anger. Using these will help reinforce learning. Some researchers believe that emotion is not a separate pathway but a factor that can enhance or shut down the other memory systems.

The truth is that there are probably memory systems that have not been discovered as yet, but for now the information about these three (or five) systems is important to helping all students to be successful.

2

Who Is
At Risk and
What Can We
Do About It?

While the criteria for labeling students as being at risk vary from school to school, the definition remains the same throughout. At-risk students are those students who, without intervention, are at high risk for failure. The important part of this definition is "without intervention." Labeling students being at risk should be a first step in finding solutions to the reasons why they are at risk and in setting up prescriptions so that appropriate intervention will take place to prevent failure.

This is much more than simply changing the way we teach them, what we teach them, or the pace of the teaching—although those things are also critical. Intervention means that we look at the whole child to determine how we can prevent failure. When we look at the whole child, we take into consideration all kinds of interventions, including health screening, counseling where appropriate, and the programs that will be the most helpful in moving the child toward a path of success. The best programs are those that work in conjunction with all of the programs offered in a school system and that make diagnoses and prescriptions based on multiple criteria. Those programs also assign an individual or individuals to monitor the progress of the student through the system.

One such program, which I had the privilege of working with in a Texas school system, is Student Support Team (SST), an umbrella for all of the special services (other than special education) offered for intervention within the school system itself. Each campus has an SST guided by a district director and staff. The definition of the program, provided by the school, is that the

> SST is a problem-solving team which is responsible for making referrals to all special programs in the school, the district, or the community that a student may need to help him or her be successful in school. Students may be referred to the program for academic and behavioral difficulties, including substance abuse, a suspected disability, inability to progress in school, and/or discipline concerns.

For this program, a case manager is appointed to walk the student and the parents through the process to obtain the most appropriate interventions for the student.

Not all schools can afford, nor do they have the staff, to set up a program like this one, but even small schools can do the following for their at-risk students:

1. Make parents and staff aware of all of the services available for intervention.

2. Gather information that includes, at a minimum, test scores, eye and hearing screenings, doctor's notes sent to the school, anecdotal notes from previous teachers and classes, and any other testing that may have been done either inside or outside the school.

3. Assign someone to be responsible for the student so that he or she does not fall through the cracks of the system and to follow up often. We did this in a small school by assigning every teacher to a team and then giving every team 100 students for which they were responsible. They checked each week to see that none of their students were absent often, tardy to class, having discipline or behavior problems, in danger of failing, and/or in danger of not meeting the criteria for going to the next grade level. Where there was a problem, the student was called in for a conference, and then parents were called in as appropriate. We looked at the whole child. For example, if a student was not doing well in math but doing great in science, we looked to see what was being done in science that worked for this student. In this school, over 50% of the students qualified for free or reduced lunch under the national poverty guidelines and yet, within three years of intervention, we took these students to the top in terms of test scores on state and national tests and in terms of general success. As one student told me, "This school just won't let you fail."

4. Begin intervention early. National guidelines call for major intervention if a child is not reading on grade level by the fourth grade. I believe that is too late. In every school where I have been in charge of intervention, I work with principals and teachers of first graders to provide a list of the names of those students who are not reading by spring of the first-grade year. We make intervention folders for each child and we screen them for hearing and vision before going on to other interventions, including assigning an adult to read with them. Early intervention can prevent the student from further delay of essential skills in their education.

Having coordinated intervention programs for many years, I have learned to look at the hearing and vision screening first, because, many times, that is the intervention that is needed. First graders want to read, and if they are not, there is usually a specific problem preventing that from taking place. When I started this program some years ago, I was told by several of the school personnel that a particular child was just lazy and that he could read if he wanted to. I didn't agree. I have never heard a kindergartner or first grader say, "I can't wait to get to school so that I can fail." As a matter of fact, their first disappointment in school is that they don't learn to read on the first day and so can't go home and read to mom and dad.

I did vision screening on the child who was not reading and found that he had a visual perception problem (he could not read any letter that had a curve). He had been tested for special education services, but the visual perception test given to him did not contain any of the letters that he could not read. His parents took him to a noted ophthalmologist, who diagnosed the condition and fitted him with appropriate lenses. The next day in class, he read for the first time—and his classmates broke into spontaneous cheers.

How many children like him are in our schools that have not received the proper intervention?

Figure 2.1 is a chart to help you as you set up an intervention program for your school.

CONDITIONS OFTEN INCLUDED IN AT-RISK CRITERIA

The following are some of the criteria that are often used for at-risk placement. I do not include special education services here, because those will be discussed separately in Chapter 3.

ADD and ADHD

According to Sousa (2001), ADD/ADHD is a syndrome that interferes with an individual's capacity to regulate his or her activity level, inhibit behavior, and attend to tasks in developmentally appropriate ways. Sousa lists three specific indicators of ADD/ADHD: inattention, hyperactivity, and impulsivity. Since all students exhibit one or more of these

Figure 2.1   At-Risk Intervention Program

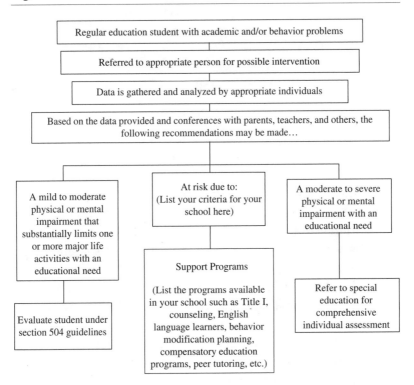

characteristics at some time, it is helpful to look at each characteristic in terms of how it is manifest in students with ADD/ADHD.

- *Inattention*—Students who have this characteristic have difficulty focusing on a task long enough to finish. They lose things easily and seem to be disorganized. Teachers often complain that the student does not listen and has difficulty getting started on procedural tasks— and even more difficulty completing them.
- *Hyperactivity*—Hyperactive students seem to fidget constantly and may find excuses for leaving their seats throughout the class time. These students also talk a great deal during class. Sitting and listening is a problem for them.

- *Impulsivity*—Students who demonstrate impulsivity do not finish tasks, especially when they encounter any difficulty and often blurt out answers when it is not their turn to speak.

Armstrong (1999) lists the following items as characteristics of ADD/ADHD:

- ADD/ADHD is most probably a genetic disorder.
- The primary symptoms of the syndrome are hyperactivity, impulsivity, and distractibility. A student may show some of these symptoms or all of them.
- ADD/ADHD affects 3%–5% of all children and adults in the United States. Some scientists believe that number is low because girls with this disorder sometimes go undiagnosed.
- ADD/ADHD can be assessed through medical history, observations, the use of rating scales to document observations, and the students as they complete performance tasks. Psychological tests are sometimes used as well to assess memory, learning, and related areas of how the student functions in given situations.
- Many students are treated with medication, although this has become a subject of controversy over the last few years.

According to Sousa (2001), ADD/ADHD students are usually between the ages of 9 and 17, are about two to three times more likely to be male than female, and encompass about 4.1% of the youths in their age group. Students reviewed for this syndrome must exhibit six or more of the symptoms for inattention or for hyperactivity–impulsivity for at least six months and those symptoms must appear before the age of seven. The handbook of symptoms is the *Diagnostic and Statistical Manual of Mental Disorders, Fourth Edition* (DSM-IV).

According to Amen (1995), ADD/ADHD students will have difficulty focusing on anything unless it is new, includes novelty, and is highly stimulating or frightening. Given (2002) says this explains why children can stay focused to video games and action-packed television programs "when they remain inattentive during calm classroom routines." Jensen (1997) makes the case that students will stay glued to video games because there is instant gratification and feedback. For students with ADD/ADHD, it may be necessary to give them specific feedback often to encourage them to continue their work. Simply saying "Good job" is not enough: The feedback must be specific and it must be constructive.

Although ADD and ADHD are often lumped together in the research, there are some basic differences between the two syndromes. According to Sousa (2001), the ADHD student makes impulsive decisions and shows off, while the ADD student is more often slow to make decisions and tends to be more socially withdrawn. The ADHD student tends to be bossy, whereas the ADD student is less assertive and tends to be polite. The ADHD student is more likely to rebel against boundaries or set structures, while the ADD student usually will honor those boundaries. The ADHD student often attracts friends to him- or herself but does not bond easily with them. The opposite is true of the ADD student, who bonds with students but does not easily attract new friends. Basically, ADD students "have no trouble sitting still or inhibiting their behavior, but they are inattentive and have great difficulty focusing" (Sousa, 2001).

Some strategies that seem to work well with ADHD and ADD students include the following:

1. Provide graphic models that help provide structure to the learning. Chapter 1 shows an example of a graphic model used in mathematics. Similar kinds of graphic models are helpful in all classes and for all ages of students.

2. Provide a daily schedule and assignment sheet in writing that has a specific place in the student's notebook. Check periodically to see that students are keeping up with this information. By checking and providing feedback, you demonstrate to students that this is an important task.

3. Use tools that bring uniqueness to the learning, such as media, pictures, graphs, music, movement, and emotion.

4. Provide opportunities for these students to experience success, and tell them when they are successful.

5. Provide specific praise.

6. Use graphic organizers that are partially filled in so that students are not overwhelmed. A tool that I especially like, from Whistler and Williams (1990), is a "story frame." Although these writers use it to help students understand the reading in language arts, the tool can be used in any subject in which students are experiencing difficulty staying on task.

7. Provide structure, a variety of media, and a lively pace. Time all activities, and tell students up front how much time they have.

8. Teach students to use mnemonics to help them remember factual information. Sousa (2001) suggests mnemonics such as "King Henry Doesn't Mind Drinking Cold Milk" for the descending order of metric prefixes: kilo-, hecto-, deca-, deci-, micro-, centi-, and milli-.

9. Limit lecture to the age of your students. None of us can sit and listen to lecture for long periods of time without fading out or becoming discipline problems. For students older than 15, a rule of thumb is to limit lecture to 20 minutes at a time; for younger students, use the age of the learners (i.e., if the learners are nine years old, limit lecture to nine minutes).

If you feel that you must provide a great deal of information to your students and that you are the only one that can do that, there are some techniques that may help to break up the lecture. One technique is called "partner exchange." After lecturing for a given amount of time, I stop and ask my students to get together with their assigned partner. I then ask partner

A to tell partner B everything that he or she can remember that I have said in the last 20 minutes. Next, I ask partner B to fill in all the information that partner A missed.

There are many variations of this tool. For example, I may put students into small groups and give an assignment to each group. One group has the responsibility of paraphrasing the information once I finish, another will think of at least five questions about the information, a third will come up with at least three key points in the information, and so forth.

Second Language Acquisition

This area of at-risk assessment goes by many names: English language learners (ELL), English as a Second Language (ESL), or second language acquisition (SLA) are some of the titles currently being used. Whatever the name, the problems are similar—these are students who do not speak the formal English used in classrooms and in the job settings of the United States. For some of our students coming from other countries, English will be not their second language but their third or fourth. For many students coming from such countries as Mexico, English is not spoken in the home or in the community; therefore, the student has opportunities to practice the language only in the classrooms and hallways of the school. The term *second language acquisition* has come about because of the need for poor inner-city students to learn to use both the language of the street and the English of the classroom and business world. Payne (2001) refers to these different versions of English as *casual register* and *formal register*.

Joos (1967) identified five kinds of language registers, which he said appear in every language. They are as follows:

- *Frozen*—Frozen language is always the same in every situation: for example, the Lord's Prayer.
- *Formal*—This is the syntax and word choice used in school and in the workplace.
- *Consultative*—This is formal register as it is used in conversation.

- *Casual*—The casual register is the language used between friends and is dependent, in part, on body language.
- *Intimate*—This is the language of lovers and also of twins. It is also the language of sexual harassment.

For students who come to us from poverty, especially the poverty of the inner cities, the speech is casual, and these students often do not know the more formal register used in the classroom. For these students, we do not want to take away the casual register that they use with their friends, but we want them to learn the more formal registers that they will need for school and for the workplace. To help these students make the transition, Payne (2001) suggests the following:

- Asking students to write first in the casual register and then to translate their writing into formal register.
- Requiring, as part of a disciplinary plan, that students express their displeasure in the formal register.
- Telling stories in both casual and formal registers, and asking students to compare the two.
- Directly teaching the formal register.

Much of what we teach (and test) in schools is declarative knowledge (i.e., factual information). In Chapter 1, I talked about the fact that most declarative information is stored in the semantic memory and that semantic memories are the most difficult to recall. Semantic memory storage is a poor retrieval choice for students who do not have the necessary language acquisition skills. For these students, use the context (e.g., storytelling and visual representations) to help these students learn factual information. Bring in a wealth of resources that are rich in visual and kinesthetic techniques to help these students gain the skills needed to learn factual information. Use movement (from the procedural memory system), context (from the episodic memory system), and emotion (from the emotional memory system) to help these students with semantic information.

Anytime we combine the memory systems, we strengthen the students' ability to store and recall the information. For vocabulary lists, teach these students to use graphic organizers, pictures, and symbols to help them remember the information. When you do this, you are providing context for the learning.

Failure to Achieve in Basic Skills

In 2002, President George W. Bush signed into law a major piece of legislation affecting all schools. The No Child Left Behind Act specifically speaks to student achievement and to the mandates on states to provide programs of substance to help all students to be successful. The act contains four key principles:

1. Stronger accountability for results

2. Greater flexibility for states, school districts, and schools in the use of federal funds

3. More choices for parents of children from disadvantaged backgrounds

4. An emphasis on teaching methods that have been demonstrated to work

Programs for students who are not achieving are specifically targeted in this act. Following are some of the programs that are specifically mentioned and their requirements.

Title I. Title I, Part A of the Elementary and Secondary Education Act (ESEA) was first passed in 1965. It was initiated in an effort to close the learning gap for students from poverty. Students identified for the program are those who are significantly behind in mathematics and/or reading. Funding is based on the percentage of students who qualify for free or reduced lunch under federal guidelines. Although being poor is not the criteria for getting into the program, the belief is that, more often than not, it is poor students who need the services.

According to a U.S. Department of Education report (2002), less than one third (29%) of all fourth-grade students performed at or above the proficient level on the National Assessment of Educational Progress (NAEP) in reading in 2000. The percentage of students reading proficiently was even lower for low-income students (13%), African Americans (10%), Hispanics (13%), students with disabilities (8%), and students with limited English proficiency (3%).

Funding for Title I is based on the percentage of students from poverty in a given school or district. However, students are served in the program based on need. In other words, just being poor does not mean that a child needs the services: The child must demonstrate a need for intervention in basic skills. This is an important distinction, because, for many years, Title I was primarily a pull-out program, in which students went to a different classroom for services. This led to the program becoming a dumping ground for students who were behavior problems, for minority students, and/or for students who needed instruction in a different modality. Consequently, many students made reverse progress.

Secretary of Education Ron Paige said at the time of the signing of the No Child Left Behind Act, "For too long, many of our schools did a good job educating some of our children. With this new law, we'll make sure we're providing all of our children with access to a high quality education" (U.S. Department of Education, 2002).

Schools may use Title I funds for one of two approaches to providing assistance: schoolwide programs and targeted assistance programs. Schools with 40% or more of their students coming from low-income families may use the funds for schoolwide programs to raise the achievement level of low-achieving students by improving instruction for the entire school. This means that Title I funds are used for all students, regardless of need. Schools that do not choose to use the funds for schoolwide programs or who do not have the percentage of low-income students to qualify as a schoolwide program employ targeted assistance programs. In this case, the funds are used for programs specifically for low-achieving students.

Under the new guidelines for Title I, by 2005–06 states must conduct yearly testing in reading and mathematics in Grades 3–8 and at least once in Grades 10–12. By 2007–08, states must also administer annual science assessments at least once in Grades 3–5 and Grades 6–9, as well as Grades 10–12. "These assessments must be aligned with state academic content and achievement standards and involve multiple measures, including measures of higher-order thinking and understanding" (U.S. Department of Education, 2002).

Additional programs targeted under Title I serve specific needs, particularly for low-income children, in an effort to close the achievement gap. Those programs and a brief definition of them include the following:

- *Reading First* (Title I, Part B, Subpart 1)—This program targets children who do not read at grade level and requires all students to read at or above grade level by Grade 3. The rule quotes information obtained from the NAEP, which shows that in 2000, about two thirds of fourth-grade classes in high-poverty schools were unable to reach the basic level of reading (U.S. Department of Education, 2002).

- *Early Reading First* (Title I, Part B, Subpart 2)—This program targets children below the age of kindergarten who may lack the cognitive, language, and early reading skills necessary to be successful in kindergarten and beyond. According to a study by the National Center for Education Statistics, "56 percent of beginning kindergartners at risk of school failure . . . cannot identify more than two or three letters of the alphabet by name, 61 percent cannot identify the beginning sound of a word, and 83 percent cannot identify the ending sound of a word" (quoted in U.S. Department of Education, 2002).

- *Even Start Family Literacy* (Title I, Part B, Subpart 3)—This program targets young children and their families in an effort to provide support in early literacy and to provide additional support to families in terms of literacy as well. There are four components to this program: early childhood education, adult education, parenting education, and parent-child activities. The program must provide summer activities as well.

- *Improving Literacy Through School Libraries* (Title I, Part B, Subpart 4)—Under this program, the improvement of literacy skills and academic achievement is enhanced by providing them with access to up-to-date school library materials, technologically advanced school library media centers, and professionally certified school library media specialists. This part of the act is based on reports by teachers that their libraries are inadequate to support the teaching/learning process and on data about the number of schools either without a librarian or without a certified librarian. Under this program, schools are required to conduct a needs assessment and to target areas in the media center that need improvement.
- *Education of Migratory Children* (Title I, Part C)— Although only about 1.4% of the students are classified as migrants, these children demonstrate many of the criteria for at-risk status, including poverty, poor health, and learning disabilities (LD). They also often carry with them the added burden of poor record keeping, disrupted school life, social isolation, and language barriers. The plan contains these requirements:

1. Identification of the needs of these students

2. Assurance that these students have the same high-quality standards, regardless of the state to which they move

3. Provision of interstate and intrastate coordination of records

4. Encouragement of family literacy standards for migrant students

- *Prevention and Intervention Programs for Children and Youths Who Are Neglected, Delinquent, or At-Risk* (Title I, Part D)—This program targets students in state correctional institutions and other state facilities in an effort to see that they are educated at an appropriate level.
- *School Dropout Prevention* (Title I, Part H)—This program's goal is to reduce dropouts in schools and is based on data that shows a dropout rate of 11% in the last decade.

Safe and Drug-Free Schools Programs. Under the No Child Left Behind Act, funds are available to schools to help in the prevention and intervention of drug use and to provide safe schools. While fewer incidents of crime have happened in the last few years, the selling of illegal drugs on school campuses and the activity of gangs has increased. The prevention programs focus on behavior.

BEHAVIORAL DISORDERS

There are many behavioral disorders in students today. For the purposes of this book, we will examine anxiety disorders and depression.

Anxiety Disorders

Anxiety disorders include phobias, panic disorder, obsessive-compulsive disorder, post-traumatic stress disorder, and generalized anxiety disorder.

Given (2002) defines anxiety as "fear of the future." While all of us experience anxiety at one time or another, those with anxiety disorders "have anxiety and feelings that are chronic and unrelenting, and that can grow progressively worse. Sometimes, their anxieties are so bad that people become housebound" (Sousa, 2001). Anxiety disorders may be categorized as—

- A phobia, either social or specific: Children with social phobia fear embarrassment when with their peers and so may avoid social contact. Specific phobias are a fear of a situation or object that is so intense that the child avoids the situation or object completely.
- Generalized anxiety disorder, which occurs in children who always expect the worst. Their fear is not based on past experience or proof that the negative effect will actually occur.
- Panic disorder, which occurs without warning and the symptoms include dizziness, rapid heartbeat, chest pain, and abdominal distress.
- Obsessive-compulsive disorder, which occurs when a child repeats a thought or behavior which he or she has no control to stop. An example is washing ones hands repeatedly or counting. Sousa (2001) says that this disorder is rare in children, but that the chances for the disorder increase at adolescence.
- Post-traumatic stress disorder, which occurs in the form of flashbacks or other symptoms in children who have experienced a traumatic event.

While we do not know all the answers about these disorders, we do know that they seem to relate to the inability of the thought processes and emotions to control the responses. Our species has survived partly because our brains were designed to shut down all unnecessary processes in the face of threat. Students who have lived under threat over time will often continue to react in a fight-or-flight mode when noises or experiences similar to past events are thrown up to them—even though threat is no longer present. For example, students who have lived in war zones may continue to duck for cover when they hear a plane fly nearby.

Depression Disorder

The number of children with depression has been rising in recent years and, with the pressures on children today, there seems to be little chance of the numbers dwindling in the near future. A study by the National Institute of Mental Health (NIMH, 2000) states that about 6% of 9- to 17-year-olds have major depression. According to Sousa (2001), children with learning problems are more likely to be depressed. These children are also at risk for illness and for social difficulties with peers and adults alike. This group is more likely to participate in substance abuse and possibly attempt suicide.

Children with signs of depression need intervention from the school through the counselor, school nurse, and other available services. In the classroom, they need an environment that is nurturing and that provides opportunities for success. They need feedback often, and they need to have opportunities to be successful so that they build self-efficacy. Teachers who include goal setting and direct instruction on how to delay gratification to complete projects help these students to be more successful.

Sousa (2001) lists some of the symptoms of depression in students. The following list is adapted from his work:

- Consistent moods that indicate sadness, irritation, and or thoughts of suicide
- Either too much or too little sleep
- Significant change in body weight and/or appetite
- Substance abuse
- Isolation from peers
- Low energy and low motivation
- Difficulty concentrating and loss of interest in even the activities the child once liked

TEACHING AND LEARNING STRATEGIES THAT HAVE A PROFOUND EFFECT ON AT-RISK LEARNING

In a study completed by Mid-continent Research for Education and Learning (McREL, 2002), undertaken in conjunction with the U.S. Department of Education, five educational practices were found to influence the success of at-risk students.

Tutoring

Most of the research conducted in the McREL study was in the area of literacy with young children. The conclusion was that tutoring could be an effective approach to serving at-risk students, provided the following steps are taken:

- Adult tutors are appropriately trained to work with the students.
- A program implementer oversees the project so that changes can be made as needed.
- Tutors have a strong belief system about what they are doing.
- There is both a diagnostic and prescriptive phase to the tutoring.

Peer Tutoring

Peer tutoring is defined as "the individualized instruction of one student by another" (Ehly, 1986). In the studies conducted for the report by McREL (2002) on students from low-income families considered to be at risk, peer tutoring had a positive effect on learning, particularly in mathematics, spelling, and reading. In any tutoring situation, there are some key ingredients in making the practice successful. Some of those ingredients are as follows:

- Structure for the tutoring with specific directions by the teacher
- Careful monitoring by the teacher
- Preparation given to students about how to carry out the tutoring activities
- Immediate and specific teacher feedback

Computer-Assisted Instruction

Computer-assisted instruction is "a process in which a computer is used to present instructional material, monitor the progress of learning, and select additional teaching materials in view of a learner's present level of performance" (Kestner,

1989; see also Hessemer, 1986). For the purposes of its study, McREL (2002) reviewed the results of 25 studies on the effect of computer-assisted instruction on at-risk students. A meta-analysis method was used to determine effectiveness. (Meta-analysis is "a research method that examines the results of a number of students in order to determine the average effect of a given intervention and identify moderating. Only research that uses quantitative methods can be included in a meta-analysis" [McREL, 2002].) The overall meta-analysis showed that using computer-assisted instruction for at-risk students on average raised the scores of students 37 points. The results seem to be more significant in mathematics and then in reading.

General Instruction Techniques

In studies based on a constructivist approach (in which emphasis is placed on meaning and understanding), the results were positive for at-risk students. In Chapter 1, I discussed the importance of meaning to the brain in learning and some ways that the classroom teacher can generate meaning. *What Every Teacher Should Know About Effective Teaching Strategies* (Tileston, 2004a) also discusses in detail how to give meaning and understanding to the learning.

Grouping Strategies

Cooperative-learning settings, in which students are put into heterogeneous groups to practice the learning, were found to have positive effects on student achievement for at-risk learners.

STRATEGIES THAT IMPACT
THE LEARNING OF ALL STUDENTS

According to the McREL (2002) study, "Marzano's 1998 meta-analysis identified nine instructional strategies that improve achievement of the general population for K–12 students. It is possible that strategies found to work for all students might also work for the subgroup of low-achieving or at-risk students."

With that in mind, here are some of the strategies identified by Marzano (1998) and Marzano, Pickering, and Pollock (2001) as having a strong effect on all students' learning with a brief explanation of each.

Prior Knowledge

Activating prior knowledge refers to the processes utilized to introduce new material in the classroom. In Chapter 1, I related that the brain likes patterns and that it seeks connections any time new information is presented. Prior to introducing new information, provide students with specific ways to think about the new knowledge. Here are a few ways to do this in the classroom:

- Use a KWKL (Know-Want to Know-Learned) graphic model to help students identify what they already know about the subject under the K and what they need to know or want to know under the W. Then, after the learning, ask students what they know now that they did not know at the beginning of the lesson under the L.
- Ask questions to get students thinking about the new learning. For example, prior to reading *The Great Gatsby*, you might ask students to come up with characteristics of what makes a good friend. Use that list later as you look at the characters in terms of friendship. At the elementary level, prior to reading *Ira Sleeps Over*, ask students what they would take with them to a friend's house to spend the night. See if the list made by the students contains some of the same things that Ira took with him.

Compare-and-Contrast Skills

Specifically teach students compare-and-contrast skills so that they can make connections between new knowledge and other knowledge. Figure 2.2 provides a list of the characteristics

Figure 2.2   Mind Maps for Nouns and Pronouns

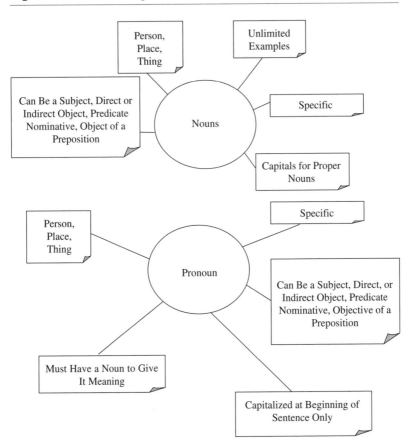

of a noun and a pronoun; Form 2.1 uses a nonlinguistic organizer to put that information into a graphic model (remember, 87% of the learners are visual). This formula can be used for anything that you want students to compare and contrast. It is also a good beginning activity to teach students to use Venn diagrams.

Linguistic and Nonlinguistic Organizers

Explicitly teach students how to use nonlinguistic (as well as linguistic) organizers to help them "see" the learning.

Form 2.1   Compare and Contrast Diagram

Noun	How They Are Alike	Pronoun
	Name a person, place, or thing	
	The person, place, or thing is specific	
	Can be the subject, direct or indirect object, object of a preposition, predicate nominative	
	How They Are Different in Regard to . . .	
All proper nouns are capitalized	Capitalization	Capitalized at beginning of sentence only
Unlimited number of examples	Limits	Limited examples
Does not need a pronoun for use	Dependence	Must relate back to a noun

Nonlinguistic organizers are graphic models that rely on the structure of the model rather than a great number of words to convey the information. Using nonlinguistic organizers was found to have a significant impact on student learning in the studies conducted by Marzano (1998).

Procedural Goals

Provide procedural goals for your students that require them to use experimental inquiry, problem solving, decision making, and investigation. Goals in most classrooms are declarative (i.e., what the students should to know) and procedural (i.e., what the students should be able to do with the learning). Providing opportunities for students to do something with the learning helps them to put the information into long-term memory. (See the information on rehearsal in Chapter 1.)

Instructional Goals

Provide students with instructional goals (in writing) and provide feedback often on how well the goals are being met. *What Every Teacher Should Know About Instructional Planning* (Tileston, 2004b) discusses this in detail. The declarative and procedural objectives of the teacher (which represent the standards) should be displayed in the classroom and should be discussed prior to the learning. From time to time, the teacher and students should review the objectives and identify where they are in terms of meeting them. For example, the objectives for a lesson to introduce the Romantic period might look like this:

Declarative objectives: Students will know . . .
- The vocabulary associated with the Romantic Period in America
- The names of some of the authors associated with the period
- The characteristics that make the writing a part of the Romantic Period

Procedural objectives: Students will be able to . . .
- Identify characteristics of the Romantic Period in given pieces of literature
- Create a nonlinguistic organizer on a selected poem

Feedback

When an instructional goal is met, provide positive feedback to the student or students. Provide opportunities in the classroom for celebrations of the learning. One of the most effective strategies for student achievement as identified by Marzano (1998) is positive and constructive feedback from the teacher and others. It is important to note here that the feedback should be merited, should be both diagnostic and prescriptive, and should be given often. Just saying "Good job" is not enough.

Student-Generated Instructional Goals

Guide students to create their own instructional goals, to develop a plan for implementation, and to learn to monitor and adjust those goals as needed. The gatekeeper to the cognitive system is the metacognitive system of the brain, which decides whether students will complete a task and the level of energy and effort that will be put into the learning. The metacognitive system is influenced by several factors, such as the self-esteem and self-efficacy of the learner.

Self-Knowledge

Help students to identify self-knowledge about their own belief systems that affect their learning. Tell students directly that they come to the classroom with a set of beliefs about the learning, about the subject, and about their own abilities that affect how successful they will be. You might conduct a whole group discussion about self-knowledge, or you might use a questionnaire such as the one below (Form 2.2).

Form 2.2   Sample Questionnaire

1. What has been your experience with [the subject area] in the past? Was it positive, negative, exciting, boring? Tell me in your own words.
2. When you heard you would be studying [the subject area], what was your reaction?
3. What could make this class interesting for you?
4. Do you like to learn by listening and taking notes? Do you prefer to learn by discussions? Would you rather learn by being involved in the learning?
5. Do you like to learn alone or in small groups?
6. How can I help you to be successful?

3

Special Education Students in the Regular Classroom

Services for students with handicapping conditions are protected by federal and state regulations and are governed by strict guidelines about planning, implementation, and follow-up. While each school district has a special education staff to assure that these students' needs are met, as the teacher of record, the classroom teacher plays a major part in the procedure. The importance of the regular classroom teacher working hand in hand with the special programs personnel cannot be emphasized enough. The best planning by the special education staff can only work when the plans are articulated and carried out by the regular classroom teacher. In order to better understand the responsibilities of the special education program, let's examine the major laws that govern this program.

FEDERAL REGULATIONS

Public Law 94-142

The beginning of federal legislation concerning students with disabilities was Public Law 94-142, passed in 1975. PL 94-142's purpose was to ensure that all children with disabilities have available to them a free and appropriate public education, which also includes special education and related services to meet their needs.

The regular education teacher should know that:

- States receiving federal support must educate children with disabilities free of charge and that the children are to be educated within the public school system, if possible.
- Each disabled child should have an individualized education plan—an IEP. An IEP must contain annual goals and short-term instructional objectives; indicate the specific special education and related services to be provided; outline the length of time those services will be provided; and specify the criteria and evaluation procedures which signify the child's educational goals are being met.
- No matter how severe a child's disability, a child cannot be refused a free, appropriate public education (known as the *zero reject concept*).
- Appropriate education ensures not only that students with disabilities are permitted to attend school, but also that an educational program will be designed to meet the student's needs, to accommodate the student's disability, and therefore to make education meaningful.
- Students with disabilities must be educated with nondisabled students to the greatest extent possible— that is, that students be placed in the *least restrictive environment* (LRE).

This law provides for certain procedural safeguards to protect the child that must be followed in all instances.

According to Public Law 105-17, Section 612 (a) (5) (A), each local education agency (LEA) shall ensure

(A) IN GENERAL.—To the maximum extent appropriate, children with disabilities, including children in public or private institutions or other care facilities, are educated with children who are not disabled, and special classes, separate schooling, or other removal of children with disabilities from the regular educational environment occurs only when the nature or severity of the disability of the child is such that education in regular classes with the use of supplementary aids and services cannot be achieved satisfactorily.

The assumption of the law for special education is that consideration for placement for services for each student with disabilities will begin in the general education classroom. To support this consideration, there are four key areas in the law:

- Supplementary aids and services are provided to enable students with disabilities to achieve satisfactorily in the general education classroom and general education curriculum.
- A continuum of alternative placements must be available in the LEA.
- The placement decision includes annual examination/ determination of the LRE.
- Students with disabilities participate with nondisabled students in nonacademic/extracurricular activities.

Individuals With Disabilities Education Act (IDEA)

Passed in October 1990, IDEA amended PL 94-142 and included the following:

- Two additional disabilities of autism and traumatic brain injury (TBI) were made eligible for special education services.

- The terminology for referring to handicapped students was changed to "children with disabilities."
- The IEPs of students 16 years of age and older must outline needed transition services, including the responsibilities of agencies outside public school. The goal of transition plans for older students is to ensure they successfully move from public school to postsecondary activities (i.e., college, trade school, employment, or independent/assisted living).

President Clinton signed the reauthorization of IDEA on June 4, 1997.

Family Educational Rights and Privacy Act of 1974 (FERPA)

Also called the Buckley Amendment, FERPA protects the privacy of parents and students with respect to student records, notices, access to and review of records, fees charged, amendment of records, hearings, redisclosure of records to others, disclosure of directory information, and complaints. As teachers, we need to be cognizant of the latest edition of this law and what we can and cannot make public or discuss with others about our students. Since interpretation changes with the times, check with your school to see what kinds of information you can share rather than waiting until a noncustodial parent comes to your door to demand information.

Americans With Disabilities Act (ADA)

ADA is not confined to children with disabilities but covers all individuals, from infants to the elderly, who are disabled. ADA is a civil rights statute that prohibits discrimination against individuals who have a disability. These protections impact employment, housing, education, and all other life-affecting opportunities. Districts not in compliance may be sued for violating the civil rights of the person with a disability. ADA went into effect during the summer of 1992.

Section 504 of the Rehabilitation Act of 1976

Section 504 is the other piece of civil rights legislation protecting a person with a disability from being discriminated against on the basis of his or her disability. According to this act, a person with a disability cannot be denied access to services or programs on the basis of the disability. The definition of a handicap under Section 504 is much broader than the definitions of disability under IDEA. Under 504, a disability (mental or physical) substantially limits a major life activity, including walking, seeing, hearing, speaking, breathing, learning, working, caring for oneself, and performing manual tests.

The provisions of this law are broader and more general than those in IDEA and do not call for the extent of services required under IDEA, but they do look at educational needs and educational accommodations for the disability. General provisions exist for notice, evaluation, and provision of supports in services if the disability results in an educational need.

Procedural Safeguards

Procedural safeguards outline the basic rights guaranteed to every child with a disability. To be eligible for special education services, a student must have a disability *and* an educational need. Why both? We should not assume that just because a student has a handicapping condition that automatically means the student would have difficulty learning. The question should be asked, "Does the handicapping condition prevent the student from reaching full learning potential?" If the answer is "yes," then the student needs the services of special education. Students who have an educational need but do not have a handicapping condition under the specified categories covered under special education may be served by the school under other federal, state, or local programs outside the umbrella of special education.

Categories of Disabilities Under Special Education

The following lists categories of disabilities as defined under special education legislation:

- Auditory Impairment (AI)
- Autism (AU)
- Deaf/Blind (DB)
- Emotional Disturbance (ED)
- Learning Disability (LD)
- Mental Retardation (MR)
- Non-Categorical Early Childhood (NCEC)
- Orthopedic Impairment (OI)
- Other Health Impairment (OHI)
- Speech Impaired (SI)
- Traumatic Brain Injury (TBI)
- Visual Impairment (VI)

EXPLANATION OF SPECIAL EDUCATION CATEGORIES

Autism

Students with the neurological disorder of autism usually develop symptoms by the age of three. These children have difficulty communicating and forming relationships with others. Autism affects 1 person in 500, and of that number 4 out of 5 are male. According to Sousa (2001), children with autism "do not interact and may avoid eye contact. They may resist attention and affection as well."

Several theories exist to explain autism, but none have been proven. One thing is known—autism appears to be a deficit in the frontal lobe of the brain, which helps us to control behavior, especially in new circumstances. Students with this disorder may become obsessive or may repeat words or phrases over and over.

The classroom teacher can assist students with autism by doing the following (based on Sousa 2001):

- Create a very structured environment for the student. Autistic students should have a place for everything and everything in its place. This may mean setting up a special notebook with folders that have specific functions—for example, a folder that holds homework assignments and a folder that holds completed work.
- Give very specific directions, in writing if possible.
- Make the assignments and the learning structured, consistent, and predictable. Autistic students do not like surprises.
- Gradually increase the opportunities for the student to be independent.
- When putting autistic students into social interaction with their peers, provide very specific directions for the activity, including what is expected in terms of dialogue.
- The educational program should be suited to the child's intellectual abilities. The environment should be very structured, and instructions must be very simple.

Learning Disabled

Students with learning disabilities have normal intelligence but do poorly in their schoolwork. A learning disabled (LD) child is not mentally retarded but has learning difficulties because of physical, emotional, or social problems. Usually, the child has had normal cultural advantages and adequate learning opportunities, yet fails to learn according to his or her abilities.

No one knows exactly what causes learning disabilities. Typically, these children do not have a history of birth trauma or negative environmental influence. They tend to develop as rapidly as their siblings, except in the area of language. Some of the characteristics of LD students are that:

- In fine motor tasks, the child has difficulty coloring, writing, or cutting and has problems establishing left- or right-handedness.

- In skills involving concentration, the child does not listen well, forgets easily, is poorly organized, and cannot follow multi-step directions.
- In reading, the student has trouble sounding out words, difficulty understanding words or concepts, and misreads letters or puts them in the wrong order.

To diagnose a learning disability, an educational diagnostician or psychologist gives a child a comprehensive assessment covering many areas (e.g., language, health, emotional/ behavior skills, sociological, and others), but the critical testing is in the areas of intelligence and academic achievement. If the child's academic achievement scores fall 16 or more points below the intelligence score and she or he is doing poorly in school, then the child could qualify as LD. An LD child may also be dyslexic or have Attention Deficit Disorder (ADD).

Within the special education population in most schools, there are more LD students than students with any other disability. Most LD students attend regular classes all day and get help from a special education teacher only when needed.

Mental Retardation

Mental retardation (MR) is often thought of in terms of the severely retarded who "look and act different." In reality, most of the persons with MR have no obvious symptoms. Through education and training, the majority of retarded persons can be self-sufficient citizens.

MR has many causes. It can occur as a result of a head injury, an illness, or because of a congenital or genetic abnormality (such as Down's syndrome). Generally, persons are considered to be retarded when they have significantly low intellectual functioning (IQ scores below 70, versus the average IQ of 90–110) and are impaired in their ability to adapt to the environment.

The functioning of persons with MR is very different depending on the severity of the retardation. The following paragraphs give general characteristics of mild, moderate, and severe/profound retardation.

Mild retardation—Mild MR is characterized by an IQ from 70 to 50—about 85% of the retarded population.

Mild MR in newborns to children 5 years old may not be noticed by the observer. However, these children are slower to walk, talk, and feed themselves than typical children. In school, these children can learn practical skills and useful reading and math abilities. They can reach academic achievement of the third-grade to sixth-grade level with special attention.

As adults, those with mild MR can learn vocational and social skills for self-maintenance (i.e., working at a competitive job and living independently).

Moderate retardation—Moderate MR is characterized by an IQ from 49 to 35—approximately 10% of the retarded population.

The infant or young child with moderate MR has noticeable delays in motor development, especially in speech, which may be limited to a few sounds or words.

The goal of education is to enhance self-help skills so those with moderate retardation are better able to function in a vocational environment. While they cannot live independently, they can care for themselves under supervision and perform repetitive, unskilled tasks. As adults, their mental age ranges from 5 to 7 years.

Severe/profound retardation—Severe or profound MR is characterized by an IQ range scores of 34 or less—approximately 5% of the retarded population.

For persons with severe or profound mental retardation, the ability to learn and care for the self is very limited. Many of these individuals, besides having MR, have other disabilities, such as seizure disorders, cerebral palsy, and hearing or visual impairment. They are able to learn basic self-help skills but have extreme difficulty learning any academic skills. The mental age of adults with severe retardation is under 5 years, and for persons with profound retardation it is under 3 years.

Educational goals for students with retardation—The key to teaching children with retardation is setting up learning situations in which they will achieve success, since they usually experience failure. Repetition is a vital element: It is important to vary the kinds of experiences, but to repeat the same concept many times. Very often, retarded children have trouble with short-term memory. Short learning sessions, well planned, can be helpful to those with a limited attention span. The more abstract the activity (e.g., learning to read), the more difficult the learning.

The major educational goal for teaching children with MR is to help them gain useful work and have adequate self-help and social skills. Thus much of their education is based on actual experiences in community settings with an abundance of practice. A multimedia approach to teaching, instead of a reliance on print-related materials, provides these students with concrete information rather than abstract ideas.

Emotional Disturbance

Students with emotional disturbance (ED) may have normal or above intelligence and would be capable of the same academic work as their peers if disruptive emotions or behaviors did not interfere. They are often frustrating and irritating to regular education teachers and classmates, because they disrupt others' learning. Students with emotional disabilities often have no friends, don't get along with teachers, react impulsively and without regard for consequences, may lose control of themselves by verbally or physically acting out, and may be depressed.

ED in students must be diagnosed by a psychologist or psychiatrist. The professional evaluator must determine the child's emotional or behavior problems have been occurring over a "long period of time" and to a "severe degree." It is very important to distinguish true ED from normal reactions to difficult situations, such as divorce, death, or other upsetting circumstances.

The characteristics of emotional disturbance are:

- An inability to have or maintain enjoyable relationships with peers or teachers
- Inappropriate types of behaviors under normal situations
- A general mood of unhappiness or depression
- Fears or physical problems associated with attending school
- An inability to learn that cannot be explained by intellectual, sensory, or health factors

Educationally, these students do best in classes with clearly defined rules and consequences. The consequences for misbehavior are consistently applied. Discipline is most effective when teachers and administrators respond in a nonemotional manner that emphasizes the connection between cause and effect. These students need close supervision during instruction and throughout the school building. Social skills training (e.g., making friends, getting along with teachers, accepting criticism, etc.) is very beneficial for students with ED in learning to act appropriately.

Students who are socially maladjusted do not meet criteria for ED.

Other Health Impairments

Students who have other health impairments (OHI) have serious health problems. The severe illness limits the student's strength, vitality, or alertness in learning situations. Children may have such serious or chronic health problems as heart disease or defect, respiratory disorders, diabetes, seizures, or cancer. The heart problem must have been diagnosed by a physician who states the condition is severe, limits the child's ability to participate in school activities, and will last a minimum of four weeks.

Orthopedic Impairment

Students with orthopedic impairments (OI) have a severe physical disability and are unable to perform normal movements because of crippling deformity. OI is diagnosed by a physician and may be the result of a congenital impairment, a birth defect, or a physical impairment caused by diseases such as polio, arthritis, or accidents.

The educational concerns for these students may include the need for additional space to maneuver a wheelchair or crutches, or the need to use a typewriter, computer, or calculator. Other considerations would be access to desks, bathrooms, and second-floor classrooms. Physical education may need to be modified or eliminated, according to the child's ability.

Speech Impairment

Language disorders range from mild speech defects, such as articulation disorders, to severe communication disorders that affect both expressive (spoken) language and receptive language (the understanding of words).

Speech impairment (SI) is determined by a speech and language pathologist. The speech pathologist diagnoses a communication disorder in one of the following areas:

- *Articulation*—The child has severe problems producing the correct sounds.
- *Language*—The child's vocabulary is severely limited; he or she may understand words, but not be able to express ideas in words or sentences.
- *Fluency*—The child has problems with stuttering.
- *Voice*—The child has difficulty with resonance, quality, pitch, and intensity.

There are more students with SI in elementary special education programs than students with any other disability. The typical speech student in elementary grades is in regular classes; the speech pathologist may offer speech therapy within the child's regular class or may instruct the child in a private setting. The typical speech student receives speech therapy for about one hour per week; the amount of time and frequency of therapy is determined by the severity of the child's disability. Autistic and MR students also benefit from speech therapy that develops their ability to communicate.

Traumatic Brain Injury

With the passage of IDEA, traumatic brain injury (TBI) was designated as a disability in 1990.

This disability is determined by a physician and is an injury to the brain caused by an external physical force resulting in total or partial functional disability and/or psychosocial impairment.

Auditory Impairment

Hearing losses can range from mild to profound, may be unilateral or bilateral, and are diagnosed by an otolaryngologist or a medical doctor. Auditory impairment (AI) occurs in approximately 1% of all children.

Treatment for hearing loss primarily consists of aids for hearing and aids for speech. The approach used most often to help a child with mild to severe hearing loss is to provide the child with a hearing aid and place him or her in the front row of a classroom. Many schools also use a total communication philosophy. With this approach, a child's language program may consist of a combination of a hearing aid, natural gestures, pantomime, sign language, finger spelling, lipreading, and body language with or without oral speech.

Visual Impairment

When visual acuity is diagnosed by a health care provider as less than 20/200 with correction, the person is considered legally blind. A person with 20/200 vision can read large-type books, while a totally blind person must rely on braille or other aids. Through the use of special technology, more and more students who are partially blind can function in the regular classroom with the use of assistance from media produced especially for them.

Deaf/Blind

The deaf/blind student has both visual impairment and auditory impairment.

Multiple Disabilities

Under the multiple disabilities category, a student must have at least two disabilities as defined under special education guidelines. For example, the student might be blind and mentally retarded.

THE PROCESS

As a classroom teacher, you will be a part of the team that provides special education services to those students who need these services. In the following paragraphs, we will walk through the process from referral to implementation.

Referral

A referral to the special education department can be made by a teacher, counselor, administrator, parent, doctor, or any other person who has knowledge of the student's needs. The referral is made in writing on referral forms provided by the special education staff. Once the special education staff receives the referral, they begin to create a paper trail to assure that all procedures are followed correctly. They must obtain permission from the parents or guardians in writing before any diagnostic testing is done. Parents are also notified in writing of their rights under federal and state guidelines.

Once parent permission is obtained, tests are ordered and a timeline is set for the process.

Do not share the information that you are given with anyone not directly associated with the education of the student. Remember that all students are protected under the Buckley Amendment and that special education students are protected again under federal legislation.

Assessment

A diagnostician or other person designated by the special education department will administer a battery of tests on the student. The assessment, together with other pertinent information, such as a health screening, eye screening, and notes from physicians, will be compiled by the special education staff so that informed decisions can be made on the educational needs of the student. Based on the results of the testing and other data gathered during this phase, the special education staff will determine the eligibility of the student for special education.

Individualized Education Plan

Based on the eligibility of the student, the student data, and other information obtained during the assessment phase, an IEP committee will meet to draft an individualized plan for the student. The committee will be made up of the parent or parents of the student, special education staff, an administrator, and teachers. The committee will determine, based on the handicapping condition, what modifications or additions need to be made in the student's learning to help him or her achieve success in the classroom. The plan may include modifications for grades, modifications for delivery of instruction, a behavioral plan, assistive technology, assessment modifications, or any other modification deemed appropriate. The IEP developed by this committee must be carried out by the classroom teacher.

Placement

The special education staff, under the direction of the IEP, will make the appropriate placement of the student. Most often, placement is in the regular education classroom for part or all of the school day. (See the definition of *inclusion* in the Vocabulary Summary and the laws that guide it.) It is imperative that the classroom teacher pays close attention to the IEP and in particular to any modifications specified in that plan. These are the guidelines for differentiation for the regular education teacher, and the teacher is required under federal legislation to follow them. Some common modifications include modifications in grades, the appearance of assignments or assessment instruments, or written outlines of the work.

Review

The IEP is subject to review by the special education staff at least one time yearly. As a classroom teacher, your input and documentation will be important as the committee makes future recommendations for the student.

4

Gifted Education

Differentiation

Differentiation for students identified for gifted services is just as important as the modifications that are made for at-risk students. In many ways, gifted students are at risk because they may not have the opportunity to fulfill their potential and may drop out mentally from sheer boredom. Those who do not drop out mentally may become discipline problems.

Being identified for gifted services means that the data shows these students need the services of a gifted program. The operative word here is "need." This is not a privilege, not an add-on; this is an identified need.

To differentiate for gifted students in the classroom, it is necessary to look at the three contexts of the teaching learning process in any given classroom: content, process, and product. For gifted students, all three processes are affected.

DIFFERENTIATING THROUGH CONTENT

Tomlinson (1999) says that, at the least, we expect all content in the classroom to be concept based, to have high relevance to our students, to contain authentic examples, to be easily transferred to long-term memory, and to be powerful. We differentiate the content for gifted learners through the kinds of media available to them and through complexity. Often, teachers who have not worked with gifted students before will try to serve gifted students by giving them more work to do. That is not gifted education; that is punishment. If a student can understand a concept by completing five examples, why give that student 30 more problems to work?

Complexity is what makes the learning different. A good example of the difference in the complexity of learning from the standpoint of a regular education student and a gifted learner may be seen by looking at how we identify the depth of our students' understanding. Wiggins and McTighe (1998) say that students who really understand can explain to the degree that they can "provide complex, insightful, and credible reasons—theories and principles, based on good evidence and argument—to explain or illuminate an event, fact, text, or idea, and provide a systematic account using helpful and vivid mental models." While this is where we hope to take all students in terms of their understanding, it is a basic expectation for all gifted students. We would further expect that the reasoning used by gifted students will be complex and insightful. To be able to accomplish this, the student will need to be exposed to a variety of materials and information, have access to the Internet, and be able to use powerful programs such as PowerPoint™ to articulate what she or he knows.

Some schools differentiate the content through content compacting, in which students who show mastery in a given area are allowed to move through the curriculum at an accelerated pace. The key here is to make sure that the students truly understand the content, not just on the surface but at a level that will serve them well in the future.

Perhaps good measures for whether any student knows the curriculum are the six facets of understanding developed by Wiggins and McTighe (1998):

- The student can explain the learning in ways that are accurate and coherent.
- The learner can interpret the information in ways that are meaningful and insightful.
- The learner can apply the information in ways that are effective and efficient.
- The learner can identify perspective in the learning that is credible and revealing and can look at the information in a way that is unusual.
- The learner can demonstrate empathy in a way that is perceptive and sensitive.
- The learner has self-knowledge and so is able to reflect on the learning and to use other metacognitive processes.

In other words, as students swim in the think tank we call school, they do more than merely treading water in the shallow end.

Some other ideas taken from Tomlinson (1999) for differentiation of content in the regular classroom include the following:

- Varying the time allowed for completion of a task
- Providing interest centers that have a wide variety of difficulty and complexity
- Using contracts so that students can sign up for work at varying levels
- Using group investigation techniques, in which students are grouped by ability and interest levels. (You would not want to do this for all activities, but gifted students do need the opportunity to work with other gifted students from time to time.)

DIFFERENTIATING THROUGH PROCESS

Process is the way in which we learn and use the information from the content. Once students are exposed to complex content, what processes can they use to learn? One of the basic ways that we tend to look at processes in school is through Bloom's Taxonomy.

Benjamin Bloom (1956) outlined layers of thought that build on each other and that become more complex as we progress through the taxonomy. The basic thought process in Bloom's Taxonomy is knowledge or knowing. The verbs that we use with the taxonomy signify the level on which we are working. Let's look at the taxonomy in terms of how it is used in differentiation in the classroom, not just for gifted students but also for all students.

Knowledge

O'Tuel and Bullard (1993) describe the knowledge level as "what one can remember from previous learning or experience. It involves simple recall and recognition; the learner may have acquired the information by rote learning." An example of a question from the knowledge level might be, "What is a noun?"

Verbs that reflect this level of understanding include the following:

- List
- Describe
- Identify
- State
- Define
- Label
- Recall

Comprehension

Comprehension occurs when students shows some degree of understanding of the information from the knowledge level. For example, at the knowledge level, students might make a timeline of the events that led to World War II, but that does not mean they understand the information. They would need to tell *why* the events led to World War II to be working in the comprehension level. O'Tuel and Bullard (1993) say that the students who can translate a math problem into a verbal problem are demonstrating this level of the taxonomy as well.

Some verbs associated with comprehension are as follows:

- Paraphrase
- Explain
- Group
- Conclude
- Restate
- Report
- Review
- Describe
- Translate
- Give examples

Application

The application level marks the beginning of higher-level thinking. At this level, the student knows the information (knowledge), has some understanding of it (comprehension), and can use the information in a situation other than the one in which it was first learned.

Some verbs for the application level include the following:

- Compute
- Organize
- Group
- Collect
- Apply
- Summarize
- Classify
- Construct
- Translate
- Dramatize
- Illustrate
- Sketch
- Solve

- Apply
- Operate
- Use

Analysis

At the analysis level, students can break information apart, analyze it, compare it, and look at the organizational sets.

O'Tuel and Bullard (1993) say, "This ability to discriminate differences is a forerunner of being ready to read." They suggest that kindergartners be given the opportunity to analyze things in terms of how they are alike and different. The organizer in Chapter 2 on nouns and pronouns is an example of an organizer designed for compare-and-contrast exercises. Kindergarten students can complete organizers using pictures instead of words.

Some verbs that we identify with the analysis level are as follows:

- Take apart
- Fill in
- Take away
- Combine
- Differentiate
- Divide
- Isolate
- Order
- Distinguish
- Dissect
- Relate
- Pattern
- Analyze
- Calculate
- Experiment
- Test
- Compare
- Contrast
- Diagram

- Debate
- Question
- Solve

Synthesis

Synthesis involves creativity, because at this level students can take information or an object apart and put it together in new and unusual ways. O'Tuel and Bullard (1993) say, that synthesis "includes the ability to organize, to arrange elements in meaningful relationships, and to make inferences about those relationships. When students write compositions, regardless of the type, they are creating something new based on what they know." Much of synthesis relies on the work of analysis.

Some of the verbs used in synthesis include the following:

- Compose
- Add to
- Predict
- Translate
- Extend
- Hypothesize
- Design
- Reconstruct
- Reorganize
- Regroup
- Systematize
- Symbolize
- Create
- Formulate
- Modify
- Minimize
- Maximize
- Connect
- Set up
- Generate
- Plan

- Design
- Create
- Organize
- Construct

How can we help students to reach the level of synthesis in the learning? All students are creative until some point in elementary school, and then their creativity seems to take a nosedive. Perhaps it is all that declarative information that we must teach by the time our students reach this grade level. Whatever the reason, there is hope, because creativity can be taught.

Alex Osborn (1963) is credited with the idea of using a checklist as a tool for helping students generate ideas. Using Osborn's checklist and adapting it, Eberle (1971) came up with a technique called SCAMPER. McIntosh and Meacham (1992) say that this technique "offers a structured way to manipulate the way students view a question, issue, or object."

Manipulating one's view often generates new and original insight. The following section provides an explanation of the acronym SCAMPER.

S—Substitute. What can you substitute to make something different? For example, fast-food restaurants have substituted chicken or fish into their traditional sandwiches (hamburgers) to add variety to their menus. In creative writing, could we substitute the point of view of the main character with that of another character in the story? What difference does it make to the story?

C—Combine. What could you combine to create your own product? Some fast-food chains combined the traditional condiments (mayonnaise, mustard, ketchup, etc.) for a "special sauce" that is a combination of those flavors. In literature, can we take the attributes that we like best from a variety of romantic heroes to create the "ideal romantic hero"?

A—*Adapt.* How can you adapt a product for a different situation? For example, for those who cannot chew, could fast-food restaurants generate a drink that tastes like a hamburger? Can we take the information on the ideal romantic hero and apply it to the real world? Are those attributes possible today?

M—*Modify, Magnify, and Minify.* Can ideas be changed so that they are larger, smaller, or modified for the purpose? Hamburger restaurants have "super-sized" their menus, they have made mini-burgers, and they have modified items by adding such things as toasted bread in the place of buns. For a problem on estimation, bring into the classroom a jar full of pennies and ask students to come up with strategies for estimating the number of pennies in the jar. Next bring in a larger or smaller jar full of pennies and see if the same theory about estimation is true when the size (or shape) changes.

P—*Put to other uses.* Can the information or the object be used for something else? Could I shellac the hamburger to use for display? How can I use my theories on estimation in other situations?

E—*Eliminate.* What can be eliminated to make the information different? Hamburger restaurants have eliminated many things to add variety to their sandwiches. For example, we can get hamburgers without onions. A student who is stumped trying to come up with a topic for an independent project might eliminate part of what he is considering to make the topic narrower. A student trying to work through a logic problem might eliminate some of the extrinsic information by drawing a line through it to help her work faster.

R—*Reverse.* What would happen if I started at the end and worked backward? Sometimes in problem solving, reversing things is a good idea: Begin with the end result and work backward to determine what went wrong. In creativity, ask, "How can I take a common object and reverse it to make something new and unique?" For example, hamburger restaurants offer hamburgers without the bun or hamburgers with additional buns in the center.

Evaluation

Considered to be the highest level of understanding, evaluation requires the ability to make judgments. An example of evaluation might be, "After studying the information on genomes and transplants, discuss your ideas about the ethics of transplanting embryonic tissue to save lives." At the elementary level, you might ask, "Was the argument provided in the poem 'Earrings,' by Judith Viorst, valid? Defend your decision. Tell why you think it was or was not a good argument."

Verbs used with this level of thinking include the following:

- Defend
- Interpret
- Verify
- Conclude
- Appraise
- Rate
- Value
- Select
- Assess
- Rate
- Judge
- Decide
- Debate
- Appraise
- Justify
- Evaluate

DIFFERENTIATING THROUGH PRODUCT

We differentiate through products by the complexity of the products that we expect from our students. For so long, in my classroom, gifted students could slop something together and turn it in knowing that it would be so much better than what the "other students" turned in that they would get a good grade. Yet I knew that my gifted students were not being challenged sufficiently. In our school, we changed all that by requiring more from our regular education students and getting it. When we did that, the gifted students began to get a run for their money. How did we do it? We did two important things: raised our expectations and provided a matrix in advance that showed our expectations for the learning.

Raising Our Expectations

First, we raised our expectations for all students. In our classrooms, we decide the lowest level on which a student can work, and the student decides the highest level. That means that any student can work at the gifted level should they choose to do so and should they demonstrate to us that they can. Students contract for the products that they will produce. Form 4.1 is an example of a contract that might be used for student work.

Table 4.1 provides a formula for putting together student projects using Bloom's Taxonomy. The verbs are the key to the difficulty and complexity of the projects. The formula involves a variety of products in terms of visual, auditory, and kinesthetic modes of learning, as well as the variety in terms of complexity.

Providing a Matrix

The second thing we did to motivate students was to provide a matrix for our students that tells them specifically what our expectations are in terms of the finished products. Again, you can differentiate for gifted students within the rubric or matrix. Table 4.2 is a rubric example that shows the levels of thought for the project.

Form 4.1   Contract for Research Project

Topic:

How I (we) chose this topic:

Initial research to be completed by _____.

Preliminary product draft to be presented by _____.

Finished product to be presented on _____.

Format in which it will be presented:

Members of the team (all team members must sign):

Teacher approval date: _____.

Checklist for teacher or evaluator only.

Initial research was completed on _____.

Product draft was completed on _____.

Final product was presented on _____.

Comments:

Table 4.1   Formula for Projects

Level of Bloom's Taxonomy	Topic	Product
Knowledge		
■ Label	Parts of the brain	Sketch
■ List	Freedoms in the Bill of Rights	Chart
■ Identify	Parts of a plant	Model
Comprehension		
■ Explain	How to perform a math operation	Letter to a new student
■ Summarize	The events that led to the fall of Hitler	Graphic organizer
■ Explain	The importance of nature to the Romantic Period	Essay
Application		
■ Demonstrate	A daily task performed by the colonists	Demonstration
■ Construct	The brain	Model
■ Classify	Information in given texts as fact or fiction	Teaching
Analysis		
■ Compare and contrast	The pilgrims' stories in *The Canterbury Tales* to the stories told by the people who frequented in the *Cheers* show	Compare/contrast diagram
■ Diagram	Information from a creative problem solving example	Diagram
Synthesis		
■ Predict	The importance of technology in the future	Short story
■ Invent	A way to help students remember vocabulary words	Teach your method to the class
Evaluation		
■ Criticize	How the policies regarding the sending of telegrams on the *Titanic* led to the disaster	Debate

Table 4.2   Rubric on Application-Level Student Project

Great	Very Good	Good	Not So Good
Able to use the information learned in a novel and difficult context	Able to use their information and skill in a variety of contexts	Able to use the information and skills in common contexts	Can only mimic what is shown
Presents the project clearly and concisely; answers all questions	Presents the project clearly with few questions	Presents the project clearly, but with some questions unanswered	Presents the project on a surface level
Uses a variety of methods (auditory, visual, and kinesthetic) to get the message across; one or more are unique approaches that show creativity	Uses a variety of methods to get the message across	Uses limited methods to get the message across or relies too heavily on one modality so that the information is not clear	Limits method to one
Project is presented on time and all steps are turned in according to schedule. All steps are completed with enthusiasm.	Project is presented on time and all steps are turned in according to schedule.	Project is presented on time and most steps are turned in according to schedule	Project is presented late and some or all steps were turned in late

Creative and Productive Thinking

While there are many, many more strategies for higher-level thinking that could be included here, there is one usually associated with gifted education that must be included: creative and productive thinking, from Paul Torrance (1979). The components of creative and productive thinking include fluency, flexibility, originality, and elaboration. While these are important to teach to all students, again, gifted students need the opportunity to use them at a high level.

Thinking skill: Fluency (generating many ideas). Fluency is a great skill to teach to all learners. In fluency, the goal is to get as many ideas on the table as possible. In the early stages of the learning process, we are not looking for quality but for quantity.

Brainstorming is one example of how to use fluency. For brainstorming, it is a good idea to set ground rules. For example, one of my ground rules is "No judging." I set this rule, because I want all ideas to be accepted at this point. I tell my students that someone may come up with something that seems like a crazy idea, but that it may lead to an idea that is viable. Also, I do not want students to put down others' ideas, because that may keep that student from participating the next time that we brainstorm. Another general rule in my classroom is that students may not say anything that they could not say to a 90-year-old woman with a heart condition.

Here are some general rules for brainstorming:

- Say what comes to mind—we want quantity.
- Do not put down the ideas of others.
- Piggyback on others' ideas.
- Everyone participates.

Here are some ways to use fluency in the classroom:

- Language arts: For an elementary lesson on *The Bear's Toothache,* by David McPhail, students can be asked to brainstorm all of the ways that you can get rid of a tooth that hurts.
- Mathematics: For a lesson on estimation, students can be asked to name ways that we use estimation in the real world.
- Social studies: Students can prepare a mind map on the ways that we influence legislation.

Figure 4.1   Flexibility: Using Categories

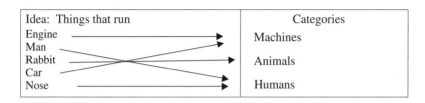

Thinking skill: Flexibility (generating many different ideas). For flexibility, students examine ideas in terms of categories to generate a variety of ideas.

For example, in fluency, the teacher might ask students to provide a list of things that are red. Students might come up with common items, such as stop sign, fire engine, and lipstick. To help students see a variety of ideas, the teacher might then ask students to provide a list of things that are red and related to transportation, to the environment, and so forth. Or the teacher might have students put together a list of things that are red, and then ask them to put the ideas into categories. Sometimes a T-chart is used to help students put information into categories. Figure 4.1 is an example of how a T-chart might be used to teach this skill.

Activities that reflect flexibility include:

- Adapting
- Combining or changing
- Eliminating
- Modifying, maximizing, or minimizing
- Putting to other uses
- Reversing or rearranging
- Speculating what would happen if . . .
- Substituting

Here are some ways to use flexibility in the classroom:

- Language arts: Have students write a new version of *Cinderella* as it might sound if told from the viewpoint of a stepsister.

- Social studies: Ask students to speculate what would happen if Americans had to find other means of transportation than the automobile.

Thinking skill: Originality. Originality involves students creating their own ideas rather than using the ideas of others.

Activities that demonstrate originality include:

- Creating a new way to do X
- Designing or inventing something
- Developing a unique process for doing X
- Giving "zany" or unusual ideas
- Imagining how one could do something
- Showing one's own ideas about something
- Suggesting diverse improvements
- Thinking of an idea that no one else has thought of today

Examples of originality in the classroom include the following:

- Science: Having students invent a new soft drink by combining flavors.
- Language arts: Having students invent a way to help others in your classroom remember their vocabulary words.

Thinking skill: Elaboration. Elaboration involves the adding of many details. Lack of elaboration is what hurts many students on essay exams.
Examples of elaboration include:

- Adding X to make Y more . . .
- Adding to
- Appending
- Building on
- Enlarging
- Extending

Form 4.2   Calendar for using Gifted Strategies in the Regular
Classroom

Skills	Sep.	Oct.	Nov.	Dec.	Jan.	Feb.	Mar.	Apr.	May
Bloom's Taxonomy									
■ Knowledge									
■ Comprehension									
■ Application									
■ Analysis									
■ Synthesis									
■ Evaluation									
Productive Thinking									
■ Fluency									
■ Flexibility									
■ Originality									
■ Elaboration									
■ Evaluation— personal									
■ Evaluation— issue									
Independent Studies									
SCAMPER									

Using Gifted Strategies

Form 4.2 provides a checklist for the teacher who wants to use gifted strategies in the regular classroom. While the strategies provided here are just a small sample of the strategies that could be used, they provide a beginning level for use in the classroom. Using the checklist, place an I in the box where the strategy is introduced, an R where it is being refined, and an M to indicate that the class has mastered the process.

Vocabulary Summary

Achievement Test

A test designed to measure a child's knowledge, skills, and understanding in subject areas. An *achievement test* measures what the child already knows.

Assessment

Assessment tests are used to diagnose student progress and assist the teacher in making informed decisions about the learning. Tomlinson (1999) says that in a differentiated classroom, "Assessment is ongoing and diagnostic. Its goal is to provide teachers day-to-day data on students' readiness for particular ideas and skills, their interests, and their learning profiles."

At-Risk

At-risk students are those students who have a higher than average probability of failure or of dropping out of school without intervention strategies. Some of the criteria for at-risk identification include low socioeconomic status, past failure, chronic illness, drug or alcohol use, and evidence of poor home environment.

Auditory Impairment

Auditory impairment (AI) is a disability in which the child has hearing problems that delay or stop him or her from developing speech, language, or academic skill.

Autism

Autism is a condition in which the child experiences severe language disorders and may display bizarre behavior, have abnormal intellectual capabilities, and have impaired social interactions.

Battery of Tests

A group of assessments given to students to determine their strengths and weaknesses is called *battery of tests*.

Bloom's Taxonomy

Developed by Benjamin Bloom, *Bloom's Taxonomy* is a list of learning skills that include knowledge, comprehension, application, analysis, synthesis, and evaluation. Because they are part of a taxonomy, each skill builds on the ones before it.

Consent

Before a child can be tested or placed in special education programs, a parent or guardian must give written permission—*consent*—for these services to take place.

Content

Content refers to the knowledge and processes that students come to know in school.

Creative and Productive Thinking

Developed by Paul Torrance (1979), *creative and productive thinking* includes fluency (many ideas), flexibility (many different ideas), originality, and evaluation.

Criteria

Criteria refers to the measurements of whether or not an educational goal is being met. For example, a criterion for spelling achievement is correctly spelling 9 out of 10 words.

Cumulative Record

All of a child's educational records are referred to as his or her *cumulative record*. The records begin when a child enters school and follow the child from school to school. It includes information about health, grades, attendance, achievement tests, and special education programs (if any).

Curriculum Compacting

Curriculum compacting is sometimes used in programs for gifted students. This modification allows students to work at a faster pace than the regular education class. As students show mastery on a skill or body of knowledge, they can move on to the next step regardless of the pace of the other students.

Deaf/Blind

Students who meet the criteria for both visual impairment and auditory impairment fall into the *deaf/blind* (DB) category. The combination of these impairments causes such severe communication and other developmental and educational problems that these students cannot be accommodated in special education programs solely for children with deafness or children with blindness.

Differentiation

A differentiated classroom provides opportunities for learners of different ability levels to be successful. The work is differentiated through the content, the process, and the product.

Due Process

Due process is a guarantee of rights and privileges that neither the government nor any other public agency can take away. For example, the right to be notified before any action can be taken concerning your child is a part of due process.

Early Childhood

Early childhood is considered to be the period from infancy to about 5 or 6 years of age. Public school education can begin at age 3 for young children with a disability as identified under the guidelines for special education. Other early childhood programs in schools are usually for children at or about ages 3–5 and are intended to help those children with language acquisition skills and the prerequisite skills for kindergarten or first grade that might not be available to them otherwise. These programs also emphasize large and small muscle development. For example, Head Start is a federally funded early childhood program for children from poverty that addresses nutrition, health, and social services.

Emotional Disturbance

Emotional disturbance (ED) is a disability in which a child's behavior interferes with his or her ability to get along with others and to learn.

Gifted Education

Programs whose purpose is to meet the special needs of talented students identified through a battery of tests as needing gifted services are called *gifted education* programs.

Guardian

A *guardian* is a person with legal authority to make decisions for a minor. The parent is the legal guardian of a minor child. A person 18 years or older does not have a guardian unless one is appointed by a court.

Homebound Program

An instructional arrangement for special education in which the teacher instructs the student at the hospital or home for a minimum of four hours a week is called a *homebound program*.

Inclusion

Inclusion is an educational philosophy in which all children with disabilities are educated in only regular education classrooms. The special services needed by the child would be provided within the regular classroom setting.

Individualized Education Plan

An *individualized education plan* (IEP) is a written plan for education and related services. It contains the educational and/or behavior goals and objectives, student competencies, the amount of special education services needed, and modifications for the regular program. The IEP is reviewed for progress each year.

Individualized Education Plan (IEP) Committee

The *IEP committee* makes decisions regarding the special education needs of a child. It determines if a child has a disability, if a special education program is needed, and if modifications in regular education are required.

Intelligence Quotient

An *intelligence quotient* (IQ) is a score that reflects a child's mental abilities and cognitive development. The IQ scores of the "average" person ranges from 90 to 110 points.

Learning Disability

A *learning disability* is one in which a child with average or above-average intelligence has significant problems in academic achievement (i.e., basic reading, reading comprehension, math calculation, math reasoning, spelling, listening comprehension, oral expression, or written expression).

Least Restrictive Environment

Employing the *least restrictive environment* (LRE) assures that a disabled child is educated to the maximum extent possible with nondisabled students.

Mainstream

A child with disabilities who is placed in all regular classes with no regularly scheduled special education services is *mainstreamed*.

Mental Age

A child's mental ability compared to children of the same chronological age provides that child's *mental age*. For example, a child with retardation may be 18 years old but have a mental age of 4 years.

Mental Retardation

Mental retardation (MR) is a disability in which a child's intellectual ability is significantly lower than the average person. IQ scores for those with MR are below 70.

Modality

Modality is the way in which we prefer to take in information. The three modalities most used in the classroom are visual, kinesthetic, and auditory. About 87% of the students in most classrooms prefer visual learning (yet we tend most often to teach using auditory methods).

Multiple Disability

Multiple disability applies when a combination of impairments occurs that is expected to continue indefinitely and that severely impairs performance in two or more of the following areas: psychomotor skills, self-care skills, communication, social and emotional development, and cognition.

Occupational Therapy

Occupational therapy (OT) is a related service to help a child develop fine motor skills. The occupational therapist may also suggest equipment to help children in daily activities.

Orthopedic Impairment

Orthopedic impairment (OI) is a disability category for children with physical challenges of the bones, joints, or muscles that affect the ability to move.

Other Health Impairment

Other health impairment (OHI) is a disability category for children with serious health problems that limit their strength, vitality, or alertness. These serious health problems may be heart disease, seizure disorders, cancer, respiratory disorders, and so forth.

Physical Therapy

Physical therapy (PT) is a related service provided to children who have difficulty using motor skills (large and fine muscles).

Process

The way in which students make sense of the learning is called *process*.

Product

Product refers to the result of the knowledge and skills of students. It is what they produce as evidence of the learning.

Public Law 94-142

Public Law 94-142 is legislation passed by the U.S. Congress guaranteeing a free, appropriate education for all disabled children.

Reinforcement

Praise or other rewards (e.g., food or toys) given to a child when he or she successfully completes a task is called *reinforcement*.

Related Service

Related services are special programs a child can receive if she or he needs special help or support in learning.

Self-Contained Classroom

An instructional arrangement in which a student receives the major portion of daily instruction from a special education teacher is called a *self-contained classroom*.

Special Education

Special education refers to those services that are additional or different from the ones provided to regular education students. The purpose is to help students who have special needs be successful.

Speech and Language Therapy

Speech and language therapy includes evaluation and instruction in articulation fluency (stuttering), voice stress, or expressive/ receptive language skills.

Speech Impairment

Speech impairment (SI) is a disability category for children having expressive and/or receptive language difficulties or with voice/fluency impairments.

Surrogate Parent

A *surrogate parent* must be appointed for any child in special education whose parents' rights have been terminated or whose parents are unknown. A surrogate parent represents the child in all the same matters that would require a natural parent.

Traumatic Brain Injury

Traumatic brain injury (TBI) is a disability category for children who have experienced an injury to the brain caused by external forces.

Visual Impairment

Visual impairment (VI) is a disability category for children with difficulties processing visual information. Partial-sighted children have a visual acuity of 20/60 with correction and can read print. Blindness is defined as central vision of 20/200 with correction or field vision (side vision) of no more than 20 degrees.

ACRONYMS ASSOCIATED WITH SPECIAL LEARNERS

ADA	Americans With Disabilities Act
ADD	Attention Deficit Disorder
ADHD	Attention Deficit With Hyperactivity Disorder
AI	Auditory impairment
APE	Adapted physical education
ARD	Admission, review, and dismissal committee
AT	Assistive technology
AU	Autism
CFR	Code of Federal Regulation
CIA	Comprehensive individual assessment
DB	Deaf/blind

DSM-IV	*Diagnostic and Statistical Manual of Mental Disorders*
EC	Early childhood
ECI	Early childhood intervention
ED	Emotional disturbance
EHA	Education for the Handicapped Act
ESL	English as a second language
FAPE	Free and appropriate public education
FERPA	Family Educational Rights and Privacy Act
FVE	Functional vision evaluation
GT	Gifted and talented (also TAG, talented and gifted)
HB	Homebound program
HI	Hearing impaired
HLS	Home language survey
ICF-MR	Intermediate care facility for the mentally retarded
IDEA	Individuals With Disabilities Education Act
IEE	Individual educational evaluation
IEP	Individualized educational plan
IQ	Intelligence quotient
LD	Learning disability
LEP	Limited English proficiency
LPAC	Language proficiency assessment committee
LRE	Least restrictive environment
MD	Multiple disabilities

MR	Mental retardation
OCR	Office of Civil Rights
OI	Orthopedic impairment
OHI	Other health impairment
OT	Occupational therapy (also occupational therapist)
PT	Physical therapy (also physical therapist)
SI	Speech impairment
TBI	Traumatic brain injury
VI	Visual impairment

Vocabulary Post-Test

A t the beginning of this book, you were given a vocabulary list and a pre-test on that vocabulary. Below are the post-test and the answer key for the vocabulary assessment.

VOCABULARY POST-TEST

Instructions: For each question given, choose the best answer or answers. More than one answer may be correct.

1. Martin Phillips is a new teacher at the ABC Middle School. Recently, while in the teachers' lounge, he heard a teacher say that she was attending an IEP meeting for a student who was LD. He quickly excused himself and went to his book on special populations so that he could look up the terms. Which of the following would he likely find?
   A. An IEP meeting is a meeting to determine the socioeconomic status of the student.
   B. An IEP meeting is a meeting to determine the best way to serve a special education student.
   C. An IEP meeting usually results in an IEP.
   D. Only special education staff attends an IEP meeting.

2. As Martin Phillips read, he found the following information to be correct:

A. LD students are no different from students served under Title I.
B. LD students are protected under PL 94-142.
C. LD students need diagnostic and prescriptive feedback.
D. LD students are usually ADD as well.

3. Students who have been identified as gifted . . .
   A. Usually do well without intervention
   B. Can be served through curriculum compacting
   C. Can be served by giving them additional work
   D. Need opportunities to work together

4. Students who are identified as LD . . .
   A. Have an IQ and an achievement level at about the same range
   B. Have an average or above-average IQ
   C. Have problems with basic skills
   D. Have low IQ scores

5. Public Law 94-142 . . .
   A. Was written to provide services to gifted children
   B. Was written for disabled children
   C. Ensures free services for special populations
   D. Ensures pull-out programs for gifted children

6. For purposes of special education placement, a child who has no parents will be assigned a . . .
   A. Guardian
   B. Special education person to represent them
   C. Surrogate parent
   D. Principal or teacher to represent them

7. Felipe is a middle school student who receives special education services. An IEP for Felipe has been given to his classroom teachers. At a minimum, Felipe can expect what?
   A. His parents signed the IEP before it was presented to the teachers.
   B. His teachers were involved in the IEP.

    C. His teachers will follow the guidelines to the letter.

    D. His goals will be reviewed every three years.

8. Martina speaks little English and is being served by a program to help her to be successful in school. What are some things that we can count on that are being done for Martina?

    A. She is served by an LPAC.

    B. She is served by an LEP program.

    C. She is served by special education.

    D. Everyone in her school has been trained to work with students like Martina.

9. Blindness is identified at . . .

    A. 20/60, with correction

    B. 20/80, with correction

    C. 20/100, with correction

    D. 20/200, with correction

10. Differentiation in the classroom is accomplished through . . .

    A. Content

    B. Process

    C. Compacting

    D. Products

11. Which of the following criteria are used to determine if a student is at risk?

    A. They are English language learners.

    B. They have low socioeconomic status.

    C. They have experienced previous failure in basic skills.

    D. Ethnicity.

12. An ADD student typically has which of the following characteristics?

    A. Shows off

    B. Is withdrawn

    C. Is bossy

    D. Is inattentive

13. An ADHD student typically has which of the following characteristics?
    A. Is bossy
    B. Shows off
    C. Does not bond with friends
    D. Is withdrawn

14. The modality most often found in school is . . .
    A. Multimodal
    B. Auditory
    C. Visual
    D. Kinesthetic

15. Second language acquisition intervention includes . . .
    A. ELL students
    B. ESL students
    C. LEP students
    D. Students who use casual register

16. IDEA . . .
    A. Is a program for gifted students
    B. Is a program for after-school services
    C. Is a federal legislation
    D. Is a program for LEP students

17. An IEP is . . .
    A. A program for after-school services
    B. A program for differentiating instruction
    C. A program for gifted students
    D. A program for Section 504 students

18. Section 504 . . .
    A. Provides services for special education students
    B. Provides services for gifted education
    C. Provides services for students outside the special education perimeters
    D. Provides services for all students

19. The definition of such disorders as ADHD comes from . . .
    A. Title I
    B. APE
    C. DSM-IV
    D. FERPA

20. The No Child Left Behind Act differs from previous legislation in that it calls for . . .
    A. Greater flexibility in the use of funds
    B. Strong research background in teaching techniques
    C. More accountability
    D. More choices for parents

Post-Test Answer Key

1. B, C

2. B, C

3. B, D

4. B, C

5. B, C

6. C

7. A, B, C

8. A, B

9. D

10. A, B, C, D

11. A, B, C

12. B, D

13. A, B, C

14. C

15. A, B, C, D

16. C

17. B

18. C

19. C

20. A, B, C, D

References

Amen, D. G. (1995). *Windows into the ADD mind: Understanding and treating attention deficit disorders in the everyday lives of children, adolescents, and adults.* Fairfield, CA: Mind Works.

Armstrong, T. (1999). *ADD/ADHD alternatives in the classroom.* Alexandria, VA: Association for Supervision and Curriculum Development.

Bloom, B. S. (1956). *Taxonomy of educational objectives, handbook I: Cognitive domain.* New York: McKay.

Eberle, R. (1971). *SCAMPER: Games for imagination development.* Buffalo, NY: D.O.K.

Ehly, S. (1986). *Peer tutoring: A guide for school psychologists.* Washington, DC: National Association of School Psychologists.

Given, B. K. (2002). *Teaching to the brain's natural learning systems.* Alexandria, VA: Association for Supervision and Curriculum Development.

Guenther, R. K. (1998). *Human cognition.* Englewood Cliffs, NJ: Prentice Hall.

Hessemer, S. J. (1986). The effect of computer-assisted instruction on motivation and achievement in fourth grade mathematics. *Dissertation Abstracts International, 47*(10A), 3705. (University Microfilms No. 8703277.)

Jensen, E. (1997). *Completing the puzzle: The brain-compatible approach to learning* (2nd ed.). Del Mar, CA: The Brain Store.

Jensen, E. (1998). *Introduction to brain-compatible learning.* Del Mar, CA: The Brain Store.

Joos, M. (1967). *The five clocks.* New York: Harcourt.

Kestner, M. K. (1989). A comparative study involving the administration of computer-managed instruction in a remedial mathematics program. *Dissertation Abstracts International, 51*(03A), 0774.

LeDoux, J. (1996). *The emotional brain: The mysterious underpinnings of emotional life.* New York: Simon & Schuster.

Marzano, R. J. (1998). *A theory-based meta-analysis of research on instruction.* Aurora, CO: Mid-continent Regional Educational Laboratory.

Marzano, R. J., Pickering, D. J., & Pollock, J. E. (2001). *Classroom instruction that works.* Alexandria, VA: Association for Supervision and Curriculum Development.

McIntosh, J., & Meacham, A. (1992). *Creative problem solving in the classroom: The educator's handbook for teaching effective problem solving skills.* Waco, TX: Prufrock.

Mid-continent Regional Educational Laboratory. (2002). *Helping at-risk students meet standards: A synthesis of evidence-based classroom practices.* Aurora, CO: Author.

National Institute of Mental Health. (2000). *Depression in children and adolescents* (NIMH Publication No. 004744). Bethesda, MD: Author. Retrieved June 6, 2003, from http://www.nimh.nih.gov/publicat/depchildresfact.cfm.

Osborn, A. (1963). *Applied imagination.* New York: Scribner.

O'Tuel, F. S., & Bullard, R. K. (1993). *Developing higher order thinking in the content areas K-12.* Pacific Grove, CA: Critical Thinking Press.

Payne, R. K. (2001). *A framework for understanding poverty.* Highlands, TX: Aha! Process Inc.

Sousa, D. (2001). *How the special needs brain learns.* Thousand Oaks, CA: Corwin Press.

Sprenger, M. (1999). *Learning and memory: The brain in action.* Alexandria, VA: Association for Supervision and Curriculum Development.

Sprenger, M. (2002). *Becoming a wiz at brain-based teaching: How to make every year your best year.* Thousand Oaks, CA: Corwin Press.

Tileston, D. W. (2000). *Ten best teaching practices: How brain research, learning styles, and standards define teaching Competencies.* Thousand Oaks, CA: Corwin Press.

Tileston, D. W. (2004a). *What every teacher should know about effective teaching strategies.* Thousand Oaks, CA: Corwin Press.

Tileston, D. W. (2004b). *What every teacher should know about instructional planning.* Thousand Oaks, CA: Corwin Press.

Tomlinson, C. A. (1999). *The differentiated classroom: Responding to the needs of all learners.* Alexandria, VA: Association for Supervision and Curriculum Development.

U.S. Department of Education. (2002). *No child left behind: A desktop reference.* Washington, DC. Author.

Whistler, N., & Williams, J. (1990). *Literature and cooperative learning: Pathway to literacy.* Sacramento, CA: Literature Co-op.

Wiggins, G., & McTighe, J. (1998). *Understanding by design.* Alexandria, VA: Association for Supervision and Curriculum Development.

Index